SUCCESS OF THE

SOUL

A 40-DAY GUIDE TO

peace
purpose
and
prosperity

SUCCESS OF THE

SOUL

A 40-DAY GUIDE TO

peace
purpose
and
prosperity

SUBAGH SINGH KHALSA

Newleaf

Newleaf
an imprint of
Gill & Macmillan Ltd
Goldenbridge
Dublin 8
with associated companies throughout the world

First published in the United States by Tuttle Publishing,
an imprint of Periplus Editions (HK) Ltd.

0 7171 2777 X

Printed in Hong Kong

A catalogue record is available for this book
from the British Library.

1 3 5 4 2

CONTENTS

MEDITATIONS AND YOGA SETS IN THIS BOOK

HOW TO USE THIS BOOK

The three qualities of peace, purpose, and prosperity that constitute the success of the soul have each been given a separate chapter in this book. I suggest that you devote a forty-day period to working with the yoga and meditations given in each chapter. The forty-day prosperity program outlined in chapter six can be done along with the exercises and meditations for prosperity in chapter five.

Each of these chapters contains basic ideas about peace, purpose, or prosperity but also presents specific kundalini yoga and meditations to enhance these qualities in you. Read through the descriptions of the exercises before practicing them, and try to do the exercises in the sequence and with the timing I suggest, as this is the way that they were originally taught by Yogi Bhajan. When you are ready to practice a meditation, read about it before finding the meditation on the tape, and then let the tape guide you through the meditation.

I can't over stress the value of establishing a daily yoga and meditation practice. You may have a hundred reasons to put off beginning until another day. You are too busy now, you need your sleep, your house is too chaotic, you don't feel well. Whatever the reason set it aside and begin now. Let spiritual practice become your norm and your spirit will guide your life.

PREFACE

I had retreated to the top of Truchas, one of the highest mountains in New Mexico. For four days I had fasted, taking no food and only an occasional sip of water from the tiny snow-fed pool I sat beside. Wrapped in my sleeping bag, I had spent hour after hour chanting in low, drawn-out tones or meditating silently. Occasionally I had slept. In the middle of the fourth night I found myself suddenly awake and sitting up, surprised at an instant transition from deep sleep to hyperalertness. I sat, empty of all thought but filled with a sense of enormous expectancy.

After a time—was it a few seconds or many minutes?—there came to me, quite literally out of the blue, the inspiration for this book; it was not just a concept or a title but an outline so detailed that it took an hour or more of writing as fast as I could to get it all down. When it had all come I was tired but so excited that I lay awake for hours considering what had happened.

The next day I left Truchas, traveling by a route that took me up and over the top of that beautiful mountain. High altitude, rocky ground, and my fasting all conspired to keep my pace slow, my mind focused on each step. At the very highest point, before beginning my descent, I paused to collect myself and pray. I asked for a sign that my vision was true, that I should write the book that had come to me. When I opened my eyes I saw on the ground at my feet a flight feather of a golden eagle.

Over the next few weeks the outline became a first draft, handwritten in a loose-leaf notebook: a book about vision, goals, and success. The book of my vision, the book you hold in your hands, speaks of the use of the meditative mind to uncover and fulfill purpose. In those first weeks of writing, however, it had become clear to me that another book should come first. I needed to begin with a basic meditation book. So I set aside my rough manuscript and over the next year wrote *Meditation for Absolutely Everyone* and recorded the audiotape that goes with it. These were published by Charles E. Tuttle Company, Inc., in 1994.

I waited another year before resuming work on this book, as I was too occupied with other matters to give the work my full attention. Now, as I write these words, I sit by another pool, the sacred tank of the Golden Temple, exactly halfway around the world from where this project began four years ago. As I finally complete this book, I do so with great satisfaction.

With this book I will share with you some of the simple ideas and powerful tools that have worked for me as I've struggled through life. I dedicate this work to all those who strive to lead lives of effectiveness, peace, and meaning. May it serve you well.

I acknowledge a particular debt to my teacher, Yogi Bhajan, master of kundalini yoga. He has been my constant inspiration and the source for all of the yoga and many of the meditations in this book. Yogi Bhajan's life exemplifies service. Much of this book exists only because of his tireless teaching.

Amritsar, India
January 1996

1
AN OVERVIEW

What can it possibly mean for the soul to succeed? Does the soul intend to accomplish something, does it have a purpose, one that we can comprehend? Can we define the soul? What might we say of the role of the individual in relation to the intent of the soul?

I have pondered these questions for my entire adult life and a good deal of my childhood. In all my years, I have arrived at only a few conclusions, a few things that I am sure of, a few things that I can claim to know. I have concluded that this phenomenon called "me" consists of a soul in the midst of a human experience, and that this soul took life in order to learn. I have concluded that I do not learn very well if I don't maintain a reasonable level of inner peace. When I become agitated or hold on to fear or anger, I haven't enough attention left over for listening, and I simply do not learn. I have concluded that I can feel little peace if I direct my energies to purposes unimportant to me. If I head in the wrong direction and take on the wrong tasks, I tend to suppress or deny the discomfort of that misdirection and pay for that denial with a loss of peacefulness and awareness. I have also concluded that when I serve the needs of my soul, when I remain peaceful and attentive while doing the "right" work, I will succeed at fulfilling my purposes.

What does it take to find peace? What would you need to do to feel peaceful right now, within your present situation? Can you imagine that? Can you imagine living as you do, with the job and home and people in your life, and still being at peace?

Many would answer that conditions would have to change before they could find peace. Their career would have to change, their health improve, their finances become solid, their children rebel less. "If only . . ." they would begin. "If only I could earn a little more, then I could begin to relax and enjoy life. Then I could find peace." Or they might begin with "When . . ." "When my teenagers go off to school . . ." Or "When I recover from this . . ." Some do not hold even that false hope: "How could I ever feel peaceful? My job makes me so miserable."

Wishing our lives away, waiting for the world to change in some way so that we can find peace or happiness: what a sad and common addiction this is. In fact, we may never know a single moment when everything feels perfect and we perceive not a single threat to that perfection. Threats to our peace constantly come at us from all sides and from within us as well. Our happiness seems threatened by others' negative opinions of us, by loss of income, by the difficult behaviors of those we love, by our body's failures, by our own emotional states, and even by the fear of losing those aspects of life that we consider desirable. In the search for happiness, we will get nowhere by asking how to establish the most ideal conditions. We must ask instead how to find happiness given the conditions in which we find ourselves.

But we do have a responsibility to *design* our lives. We can seek a career better suited to our needs and talents or choose to exercise or diet for better health. We ought to work consciously toward improved relationships with family or friends and remove ourselves from truly negative situations.

Looking forward to better times can feel wonderful. But becoming addicted to those better times and demanding them as a condition for happiness does not. We must not confuse our preferences with our needs.

Some will wonder what this state called "peace" might consist of. Perhaps they have only dim memories of times free of anxiety. I would rather guide these people into a peaceful state than try to describe it to them. We cannot reach the subjective experience of peace through talk. Let me say only that peacefulness does not imply a state free from pain or difficulty but rather a state free from suffering or agony over the *presence* of pain or difficulty. Therein lies the secret to happiness; we will return to this theme over and over throughout this book.

Some others will wonder if they really desire such a state of happiness and peace or if it wouldn't lead to laziness or lack of drive for the "good things" of life. I'll speak from my own recent experience. In the preface I mentioned that other issues had kept me from starting to write this book for a full year after the publication of my first book. During that year I sold my dental practice. Many old fears and insecurities surfaced as I negotiated the sale. Often I failed to maintain my peace in this time, and as a direct consequence I had precious little attention left over for writing. Other aspects of my life suffered as well. My physical energy dropped off, and I often experienced self-doubt, anger, and other hard emotions. I became, in a word, inefficient, and little of what I cared about most got the attention it deserved.

As I slowly recovered my peacefulness—rediscovering and using the techniques described in these pages—wonderful changes began to take place. My energy returned to normal, and I became better able to focus on my goals, which I met with greater ease than I had believed possible. Much more gets done now, and with a lot less effort. Peacefulness should not be confused with escape from the world. Quite the contrary. We require peace if we wish to truly succeed in the world.

Fortunately, many have gone before us on this quest for peace. Often the wisest have shared their wisdom, so we can learn from them and follow their example. We don't have to reinvent the wheel of peace but can use the ways that they have used. With diligence and commitment, we can experience for ourselves this thing called peace. I wrote *The Success of the Soul* to share with you specific, powerful techniques for this transformation. I want you to know how to quiet your body and mind and how to explore your own consciousness.

Purpose is a second major theme of this book. We all have a purpose, or purposes, and missions to fulfill. A friend of mine challenged this idea. She said she had no wish to have some special task she had to do in order to feel fulfilled. She talked about her wish just to do whatever she set her mind to and to do it with excellence. She spoke also of her need to have more love in her life, to have more connection with her husband and closer friendships. As we talked, I heard her describing purpose, although she was uncomfortable with that term. The deep yearnings she talked about were clues telling her where to put her attention. If she can learn to listen to herself with openness and to explore her own feelings fearlessly, she will begin to discern the directions that might be most profitable for her to take.

The process of seeking vision within yourself may become one of the most exciting and rewarding adventures of your lifetime. Like the search for peace, the quest for vision and purpose may have its difficulties, but to know your authentic self, to know where to put your energy, can prove most liberating. This vision quest goes beyond career counseling (my friend already had a career as a business consultant) and delves into the qualities and values that you most care about. It deals with incorporating those qualities and values into all that you do. For some, this implies a career change or even a more total change of life direction. For others, it has more to do with their intentions within their present careers or situations. In other words, vision concerns not only what you do but also how you do it.

These may seem obvious, simple things, but many people find them challenging. Few people know, really know, what they want. Most wander through life, taking it as it comes, hoping for good luck and cursing the bad, or drive themselves to realize goals they do not really embrace. Fortunately, you have an alternative. With effort and with the help of appropriate techniques, you can come to understand your real goals and your highest purpose. This book offers you some of those techniques. You'll need to supply the effort.

Finally, this book addresses prosperity. We'll spend some time coming to an understanding of the meaning of the word and still more time embracing the concept. For now I will only say that prosperity implies much more than a good supply of cash. You'll prosper when you follow your heart and your inner vision with peacefulness. Prosperity implies success, not merely at a career but at life itself. We will speak here of the success of the soul, the fulfilling of purpose. We won't only count as a success reaching an end point, as in "I will feel successful when I complete this book." Rather we'll measure success in how well, how joyfully, and how responsibly we proceed toward our goals. We'll find one measure of prosperity in our willingness to succeed, another in our ability to give. Prosperity, like peace and purpose, may not come easily. All three require commitment and real effort. This book explores all of these challenges and will provide you with techniques to help you along your path.

Take your time as you read this book. You may get more benefit if you read one chapter and spend some time practicing the techniques and absorbing their effects before proceeding to the next chapter. Slow yourself down. Find your quiet inner presence and dwell in that for a time. Make the practice of peace a daily thing. One does not "get" peace and then move on. As you proceed to investigate purpose and prosperity, you will want to maintain your practice of peace as well. If you find yourself hurrying to understand your purpose or rushing to "achieve prosperity," stop yourself; you have missed at least some of the point. Consider spending forty days practicing the techniques in each chapter before moving on to the next. When you've completed a 120-day cycle, begin again. Practice the qualities of peace, purpose, and prosperity continuously. Don't limit yourself by thinking of them as goals to achieve.

2
THE SOUL

How can we discover our purpose in life? How might we fulfill it? In this book I hope to shed some little light on these questions.

We'll begin this inquiry with an examination of the phenomenon called *soul*, although trying to define soul would prove futile. Any definitions I might supply would only limit your imagination, and imagination might very well prove important as you explore the realms of your soul. Rather than define the word, I will speak of the soul in functional terms, in terms of what it does or means in our lives, and in terms of its purposes. We will begin with a simple question: "Who are you?" Take a few minutes to consider your answer to this fundamental question before reading on.

In your answer, did you give a list of your personal characteristics? Did you think about what you do or that you had certain roles, that you act as a mother or father, a son or daughter, that you call yourself a student or a worker? Did you think of your race or sex or age? Did you include some of your qualities: that you see yourself as loving, or creative, or romantic? Perhaps you included thoughts you've had, feelings, or political convictions. You may have defined yourself in terms of your body and mind—as all that exists within your skin, or as some aspects of your psychological makeup.

Have you noticed that each description you apply to yourself limits you? If you call yourself disciplined, then you diminish your ability to experience your undisciplined self. If you call yourself sick, then you may not notice those healthy parts of yourself. Whatever labels you might apply to yourself tend to separate you from other possibilities. Whatever your concept of self, it becomes like a wall around you. You define as "you" all within the wall; everything else becomes "not you."

You might have also noticed that these walls can change. Today you may think of yourself as young, but soon enough you will call yourself old. Little of our defining identity remains stable throughout life. In a very real way we continuously redefine who we "are." We constantly change our self-identity. And yet doesn't someone, some self, remain unchanged in the center of all this?

Did your way of answering the question "Who are you?" take into account the times when the wall breaks down entirely and there suddenly appears a much larger sense of self? Have

you not had moments when you've experienced a greater identity, when you've experienced a oneness with another person,
with art or music, with your own creative work, with nature, or
even with the universe as a whole, times when you went beyond
your boundaries?

My questions are intended to help you recognize the existence of the soul: a truer, more fundamental self. We begin to
perceive this self as we transcend our personal selves and breach
the boundaries imposed by our more limited identity. I do not
wish to go beyond this in my description of the soul. To do so, as
I have said, would limit your imagination, and that would not
serve you. Instead, let us consider the place of this transpersonal
self in everyday life.

When we observe certain people, we say that they live in a
soulful way, appreciating life's great glories and simple pleasures
as well as its pains. Living the life of the soul, they allow themselves to experience life just as it presents itself, accepting, even
welcoming, the difficult, in much the same way that they welcome the easy. The life of the soul does not exclude humanness
and the pain that goes along with being human; rather it
embraces them. The soulful person remains joyfully grounded in
the present, in the here and now, close to life (and yet ever
mindful of the spiritual). The soulful person lives with heart and
feeling.

Soulful people recognize as right whatever their life might
consist of, whatever they have been given to experience. But how
can I consider "right" the death of a loved one, the loss of a job,
or life in an abusive relationship? I certainly do not mean that

these situations are desirable. Nor do I mean that they are deserved. By "right" I mean that one can work with, can learn from, the circumstances one finds oneself in at this moment and that these circumstances can prove useful in the search for meaning. We find difficult only those situations that touch us where we remain underdeveloped, where we have not yet found peace, where we still have more to learn.

Can something like the death or suffering of one we love ever not cause us to suffer along with them? Can we, should we, somehow come to find such a thing acceptable? Yes, we can. Soulful people do come to grips even with suffering and death. They experience pain and loss and grief, but they do not continually rebel against the existence of pain or death, and so they do not suffer in the same way. Pain inevitably comes to every life. We will all experience times of loss or rejection or will injure ourselves or become ill. But we suffer, as I am using this word, only when we wish that the pain would not exist, when we demand that the universe would somehow treat us differently. Desire increases our suffering and acceptance decreases it. Certainly no one would prefer pain to pleasure, but we need not reject pain so strongly as to create suffering.

We know this intuitively. We know this in our souls. But many of us don't hear the voice of our intuition or see with eyes of soulfulness, so we live in constant rebellion against this basic truth. The suffering we feel constitutes evidence of a rift between our finite self and a wise inner sage. But soulful spirituality, growing in part out of our everyday human difficulties, can show us the way to heal that rift and bring the personal self into an alignment with the purposes of the soul. In this we find the fundamental work of life. To ignore it means that the suffering will go on and on.

Although we may acknowledge the existence of the soul, as a culture we seem to give less and less serious consideration to the needs of the soul in everyday life, including even in our spiritual or religious life. For example, we build sterile steel-and-glass structures for offices and build factories made to house machines, not people. In such places spontaneous imagination and creativity seem out of place, and in them we blindly accept the brutality of soulless work, submitting to high-stress careers or work without meaning.

Many of the foods we eat have been stripped of all individuality. We remove the germ, the very soul, of our wheat, then process it into pale loaves and package it in plastic. When we finally eat this stuff with bologna or processed cheese (products that are similarly far removed from their original selves), we nurture our souls no more than we nourish our bodies.

When sick or injured, we tend to ignore the soul and seek cures only through physical means. Clinicians attempt to control the body with external forces, applied to anything from the muscles and joints to the molecular structure of the chemicals of the brain. We ask only "What has gone wrong?" and "How can it be fixed?" Only rarely do we also query, as a shaman might, "What does the soul need to have happen here?"

Often, a terrible rightness lies hidden within our symptoms. Once when I was still a practicing dentist I injured my right shoulder in a motorcycle accident. The injury made reaching my arm across my chest quite painful. One of the few activities this interfered with was my work as a dentist.

The symptom persisted for weeks until one day, in my meditation, I began to examine carefully what I had done to myself. After a time I recognized that I had injured myself as a way to avoid practicing dentistry. I began right then to reexamine my career and give serious consideration to ways of practicing more in keeping with the needs of my soul. After this my arm rapidly regained its range of motion, and within two days it was completely healed. My soul apparently used the injury to communicate its needs to my conscious mind. Don't we have a responsibility to listen to such communication? Shouldn't we welcome, not kill, the messenger illness, and so learn from it whatever we can?

Just as buildings, food, and health care can lack soul, so too can even our spiritual and religious lives. On one extreme, religion may contain nothing more than a weekly helping of platitudes served up on a dish of meaningless ritual. At the other extreme, spirituality may separate us from the everyday, causing us to chase after fantasies of salvation while losing sight of life itself. Spirituality of this ilk tries to rise above body and mind to find God, whereas a soulful spirituality speaks to our deepest longings for elevation of consciousness but does not ignore body, mind, or the more hidden aspects of our being. By ignoring or denying, in our spiritual quest, the pleasures and pains of the everyday self we run the risk of creating a "spiritual" life that is irrelevant to the real world.

Appreciating a great work of humankind—a cathedral or a

rock garden, a symphony or the thin note of a bamboo flute—reminds us of the soul. Truly appreciating nature or the laugh of a friend recollects God. Each of these experiences, when we allow it to fully touch us, becomes a way inward, in toward the soul. All human experience, difficult or delightful, can serve us in this way. We need only to open ourselves to the experience, without interference from the critical mind, which judges one thing as good and another as bad. The completion, the deep satisfaction in this, can come only when we allow ourselves to fully experience each event of our lives.

When the sister of a friend died after a long and difficult illness, my friend deeply felt a whole range of emotions. She intimately knew the sadness, the loss, and the sense of missing her sister. She felt her exquisite pain as only she could, and she did not retreat from it. Sometimes she would briefly forget her grief and busy herself with family and career, but she did not bury her pain. When she felt ready she again let herself feel the full force of her emotions. Talking of her sister, she often would cry. Sometimes she would apologize for her tears, but I never saw that anyone was bothered by what she went through. All of us around her during that time appreciated the healing and growth that came about through her soulful acceptance of her experience and all of her emotions.

We wish, in the wisest parts of ourselves, to gain even more wisdom, to know life in all its richness, to experience all aspects of life without fear or avoidance, and to welcome whatever lessons it might teach. Presented with a difficult situation—the death of a loved one or a disagreement with a clerk in a store—

we might react in any number of ways. On one end of the spectrum, we've all had reactions of anger, fear, or resentment, of demanding that the situation change to our liking, now. On the other end of the spectrum, we might welcome the situation as one more invitation from our soul to see the true nature of our selves and to grow from that seeing. In situations filled with hard emotions, the most fulfilling responses leave all involved with a feeling of completeness, of somehow healing or becoming more whole for having gone through it. I yearn (I think we all do) for the sense that my responses served the needs of my soul and the souls of others. When I don't serve my soul in this way, I feel frustrated and angry at myself. I want a chance to relive the experience, to make it right.

Have you noticed the tendency to have similar difficult experiences over and over? A woman may remove herself from an abusive relationship only to find herself in a similar one soon after. We keep getting into the same argument with our partner. We feel hurt, time after time, by the same sorts of thoughtless behavior, while some other types of thoughtlessness we hardly notice. We seem to relive what we haven't yet mastered, suffering this year in the same ways that we did last year, doing it over and over until we get it right.

As an alternative to prolonging our suffering, we can fully embrace the difficult—so much easier to say than to do! We have this time on earth to learn whatever lessons life brings our way. When we try to avoid the lessons, through a strategy of denial or negativity, we can rest assured of another precious learning opportunity soon. Suffering provides us with a signpost.

It points in the direction where we can grow in understanding. The pains of life, just as much as our passions, guide us to the experience of our soul.

The soul by its nature must learn. It chooses certain incarnations, life circumstances, and experiences in order to proceed along its evolutionary path. This learning soul needs a mind and a body. It needs the experiences of the individual in order to grow. Soul and personality function together in a collaborative learning relationship, each needing the capacities of the other to complete its task. When we understand this symbiosis, this synergy between the finite and the unlimited, we can free ourselves from resentment about the circumstances of our life. We have what we need.

Let soulfulness become the very foundation of your spiritual life. We cannot expect to experience our soul or transcend the personal unless we accept the personal. Once that acceptance has occurred, and not before, we can participate in the most magnificent of all adventures, the exploration of the territory of the soul. In the next chapters we will see how to do this and how to bring our discoveries back into everyday life.

3
PEACE

Desire, the very opposite of peace, infects us like a plague, a universal disease, causing universal suffering. We all suffer, and, sadly, we believe in the specialness of our own suffering, the validity of it. We each demand, indignantly, that the universe treat us differently and that the causes of our pain disappear, evaporating like a mist in the morning sun. Somehow we should have more pleasure, a better marriage, more security, and less hardship. This you will recognize as the common view. It says that things should go our way, and that we shall find happiness if and when certain conditions change for the better and even then only if other, more desirable, conditions remain in place. This view wants more of this, less of that, and constant improvement. This view does not tolerate setback or adversity but reacts to them with anger and resentment.

A rarer view finds the difficulties of life tolerable, something to work with, and sees little gain in railing against one's fate. It understands that we might better use our energy to correct or get out of the difficulties we face and to avoid similar problems in the future. By rising to life's challenges, the holders of this view can begin to create the better lives they desire. And yet this view does not bring lasting freedom from suffering. For the holders of this view, happiness remains dependent on improvement, a precarious stance indeed. We simply cannot control everything that might spoil our chances for constant improvement and ever greater happiness.

A still rarer attitude understands difficulties as a part of the richness of life, as gifts, as opportunities for learning. The holders of this uncommon view are blessed with an ability to turn the inevitable hardships of life to their own advantage. These people remain positive and see, even in catastrophes, ways to grow and to experience more of the fullness of life. For these blessed people, disaster equals challenge, and challenge well met gives meaning to life. They know that difficulties met with a positive attitude can serve as some of life's greatest teachers.

The rarest attitude of all views pain and pleasure as the same. Only those few who do not become attached to a preference for the pleasurable over the painful or the friend over the enemy know true peace. Throughout history, those who have achieved this remarkable state have been held in the highest esteem. These saints and sages serve as beacons to guide others toward fulfillment. They know that only by fully embracing everything that life offers can one find peace. There can be no other way.

Of course, we put ourselves at some risk if we hold out the world's precious few true spiritual masters as examples of whom we might become. Perfection, if not exactly a fantasy, does remain virtually unattainable. I know earnest people, people who have never believed themselves good enough and whose minds remain filled with early memories of criticism or abandonment, who cannot enjoy themselves because of a painful awareness of their own imperfections. We must not demand of ourselves that we also excel at peacefulness!

Fortunately, we need not think of peace as an all-or-nothing affair. We can easily imagine a spectrum of peace with the perfection of the spiritual master at one far distant end. We can only start here (wherever we now find ourselves along the continuum) with all of our passions and imperfections. We can make peacefulness the work of this moment, the game of life that we play. For we can do no more than let go of our desire for perfection, just as we let go of other desire, and hold instead to a simple inclination toward peace and a humble awareness of our fears.

The examples of the great masters give us sure knowledge that humans do not have to suffer, that an awakening can occur, and that we can participate (if we choose) in the joy and freedom of inner peace. But their example also shows us that this freedom comes with a cost. Most of us will purchase it a little at a time, over many years or over an entire lifetime, with the coin of disciplined spiritual practice and with ever-increasing awareness. Attaining this freedom will require a great deal of us. There will be no reliable shortcuts and, as Yogi Bhajan says, "No liberation without labor."

Of what, then, does this labor consist? By what methods might we learn peace? The answers are both daunting in their complexity and surprising in their simplicity. The complexity results from how complex we have become during the course of our lives. If you intend to embrace all of life, you will have to confront what you have made of yourself, including the secret self that slowly evolved and has heretofore remained largely hidden from the awareness of your conscious mind. Over the years of your life, you have learned intricate responses to the world, repeating patterns of defense and withdrawal, aggression and engagement. To learn peace you must allow yourself to see these, exposing to the clear light of awareness each of your reactions, even the most subtle.

The complexity of our environment also complicates the work of peace. We each exist in the center of a busy web of relationships, and we have our home life, careers, and recreation. We live in bodies that give us pleasure and pain and countless impressions of the inner and outer worlds. Furthermore, the outer world itself has grown in complexity during the course of our lives. All of this stimulation multiplied by the intricacies of our personalities produces an endless supply of objects for our awareness.

And yet, despite the complexity of what we have to work with, peacefulness remains essentially simple. Regardless of what we experience, we need only to hold it in nonjudgmental awareness and we will know peace. Simple? Yes, but definitely not simplistic. With mindfulness, as we call this approach, we will gloss over nothing, ignore nothing, as we free ourselves from suffering in the clutches of desire.

Rather than discuss these themes at length, I prefer now to help you to have an experience of peace through the medium of meditation. Ultimately, only the paths of love and meditation have the power to take you to the place of peace, and there is no reason to postpone setting out on our way. Later there will be plenty of time to evaluate the voyage with the knowledge that can come only from experience.

MEDITATION 1: MINDFULNESS
(TAPE 2, SIDE 1)

Let us now explore mindfulness as a specific technique. You will need to find a quiet place where you can sit undisturbed for a few minutes. The opening segment on Side 1 of Tape 2, which comes with this book, will guide you through your first meditation sessions. Later you may want to practice without the tape, so you will have more freedom in when and where you practice and for how long, but for now use the tape and let it help you to get started. Even if you already have a meditation practice, use the tape a few times to experience this particular meditation style. Later, when I introduce additional techniques, this simple awareness meditation will serve as your foundation.

I've kept the instructions on the tape brief so I will preview them here in some detail.

Sit so that you hold your spine straight but not rigid. You may use a straight, firm chair if you find sitting cross-legged on the floor uncomfortable, but avoid an easy chair or couch as they will not let you sit in an erect, dignified posture. If you can sit without leaning against the back of your chair, so much the better. Whatever your choice, aim to sit with a straight spine, leaning neither right nor left, forward nor backward, in a relaxed and comfortable posture.

If you sit on the floor, a cushion might help. Sit on the front of the cushion so that you can raise your hips in relation to your knees. If you use a chair, keep both feet flat on the floor, legs uncrossed.

For this meditation, simply place your hands in your lap, palms facing upward. Then close your eyes and allow the tape to guide you through the meditation. After the guided meditation, turn off the tape and sit, meditating on your own for as long as you wish.

Do all this now, before reading on. Begin your meditation practice today. This moment marks a new beginning in coming to know your true self, but don't expect lasting results from one or two meditation sessions. You will pursue awareness over your lifetime, as an attitude that needs consistent cultivation, as a constantly renewed expression of your liberated self. The power of meditation comes from its repetition, so keep practicing.

❧

Now that you have begun to experience the effects of this meditation, we can discuss some of its ramifications. Fundamentally mindfulness tells us to drop the possibility, and even the desirability, of eliminating the mind's activity or the body's sensations and feelings. On the contrary, you will come to see that it is very possible, and highly liberating, to embrace the full content of the body and mind. If we do not welcome even the painful and difficult things that we experience, then we must reject them, wishing that they were not there, that we did not have to feel whatever we find difficult. Thus begins suffering, anxiety, and emotional stress. By embracing the fullness of our experience, we gain personal power through our lives. Otherwise we put ourselves in the difficult position of trying to gain power over life, a pursuit ultimately doomed to failure.

Don't wonder, "What shall I do about my life?" Rather ask, "What shall I do with my life?" The mental, emotional, and even physical discomforts we experience can become the medium through which we examine and ultimately heal and regenerate both ourselves and the outer world. No program for self-help (or social, political, or economic improvement, for that matter) will make significant gains if it does not include fundamental changes in consciousness. Without such change we can only rearrange the elements we face; we cannot get beyond them.

We can learn to accept problems and difficulties as gifts to work with. The problem-solving mode of self-help, so popular today, often seeks shortcuts to get around or beyond our problems. We rarely get to go into our problems, to face our difficulties squarely. We want to ignore these forces as if they had no substance, no message or meaning to give us. But these forces are real, and we cannot ignore them without cutting off a part of ourselves. To push on toward our goals despite our feelings will serve us no better than to dwell endlessly on our bad parts or our mistakes or ill fortune. Instead of either of these alternatives, we can find a middle way, one where we choose to face ourselves as we are. In this way we understand each interaction, each event of life as being exactly what we need for our growth at that moment. When used in this manner, the thoughts and emotions engendered by the events of life, whether "good" or "bad," have no power over us; in fact, they become the very tools with which we work.

In your meditation, allow each sensation, thought, or emotion to arise as a part of your consciousness. Judge nothing, accept everything, exclude nothing. Let go of attachment to the needs of your personal self (for safety, love, comfort, and so forth) and ally yourself instead with your authentic needs, the needs of your soul.

When you examine them, you will find that the needs and desires of your personal self, things such as security, good reputation, physical comfort, and good health, are often the very barriers you face in creating or having all you might hope for. If, for example, I have made a serious mistake and I try to hide it to protect my job or reputation or so as not to appear foolish, the denial (not the mistake itself) becomes an obstacle in my path. My personal self's need to look good stands in opposition to my soul's need to learn and to experience peace. The denial becomes painful: It hides away a part of myself, telling me of my inadequacy. Its continued existence creates tension in my body and mind. If I wish to serve my soul, I must let go of my denial and embrace the foolish part of myself that made the mistake to begin with. In my meditation I can allow the feelings conjured up by my mistake just to lie there, fully felt, but without judgment and without even giving the feelings a name.

The same holds true for the pleasant. We can become addicted to and intoxicated by the desirable. If, instead of making a mistake, I have done some good deed and have become the object of admiration and honor, the pleasure of that may captivate my mind. I could simply experience the pleasure of the moment and then let it go, or I could dwell on how fine I must appear, imagine future honors, and allow my head to swell with pride. Some of the fundamental effects of this intoxication resemble the effects of denial. In both cases, I lose my self, forgetting my true nature. In both cases, I concern myself more with my appearance than with my actual state. And, in both cases, I look for control over pleasure or pain where I can have no real control. This attempt to control lies at the root of suffering.

Ultimately, we want happiness, and that means that we want to give up our suffering and live in higher consciousness. But we cannot give up what we do not have. In order to let go of our difficult feelings, we must first accept them. We do this work in meditation. We use meditation as the technique to feel ourselves fully. As this occurs, healing comes spontaneously and rapidly, and transcendence beyond our limited self begins. This magic results from nothing more than our attentiveness.

When we meditate honestly, we see many things about ourselves that we may not like. If the contents of our minds were somehow projected onto a screen for public view, I think we would all suffer embarrassment and shame. In our minds we lust after one thing and fear another. We greedily want to keep the pleasure coming while we shun the unpleasant. We all have moments of anger and pride. We all have our secret desires.

Mindful meditation focuses our awareness on this everyday mind of ours and begins to separate out our reactions, positive and negative, from the sensory events that preceded them. We begin our practice and our search for peace, purpose, and prosperity with an awareness of self: our bodies, feelings, and thoughts as they are at this moment. We then allow that awareness to continue as we become especially aware of our breath. Holding to the awareness of breath, we watch the endless parade of sensations and thoughts and our reactions to them. Slowly, behind all the sensations and thoughts, we become aware of consciousness itself. Here we examine this "I" we have been so protective of, so identified with. Eventually the sense of a separate, reactive self disappears, and we reach the natural state, the state of peace, unsullied by desire and not attached to a false sense of self.

A woman in one of my classes told me that speaking publicly, while not impossible for her, always filled her with a sense of panic. She knew exactly why. When she was six years old, her family had moved to the United States from France, and at first she knew no English. At school her awkward moments in front of the class, taught by an unsympathetic teacher, embarrassed her intensely. Over time she learned to compensate for her feelings of panic, but they remained hidden in her nevertheless. She chose to try to ignore or "go beyond" her feelings. Although she had gotten by, the strong, half-buried feelings of discomfort had never abated.

I urged her to allow the feeling of panic into her meditation, to experience it fully, not to try to wish away a part of herself but to embrace it. This radically different approach led to a healing of her old wound. The feelings of panic decreased and eventually disappeared altogether as she allowed herself to feel her discomfort rather than hide it away.

When we experience emotional or physical trauma, defended areas of dread may remain hidden away within our minds or bodies. We recoil when we get too close to one of these secret places where fear has taken hold. Meditation gives us the power to examine these places, to see them clearly. Meditation acts like a torch to illuminate the dark recesses of our minds.

Through our meditation, these stored and hidden feelings, these dark areas that can cause so much suffering, can become the means of our release. Whenever you feel discomfort, consider it as a signpost pointing directly toward a defended area. Honestly follow the path that sign indicates and you will rediscover an old wound. Put all your attention there for—although this may seem to fly in the face of instinct—whatever we experience with clarity and directness cannot hurt us.

We need, simply, to change our perception. We need to embrace, rather than flee, our wounded, neurotic self if we wish to find the enlightened self within. We should not allow the recesses of our minds to harbor dark, unexamined, unassimilated bits of consciousness. The possibility of being whole and healed does not exist for us as long as we reject a fragment of ourselves, no matter how ugly or fearsome it may seem. Our unassimilated parts require defenses (so that no one, ourselves included, will see them), and defenses prevent satisfying contact with ourselves, with others, and with the world around us. Emotional and physical discomforts, including injuries and diseases, show us where to look to find the defended parts. It is here, face to face with our pain, that we do the work of meditation, the work of healing and becoming peaceful, the work of unflinchingly studying the self, whatever we may find.

This work of awareness will never end, no matter how long we maintain our meditation practice. Mindfulness, after all, does not try to change but simply to allow. It exposes to our consciousness all things, making no distinction between the delightful and the grotesque, and gives us a way to live with ourselves in peace.

And yet this brings up a sensitive and critical issue. At what point might we choose to transcend our feelings, to forget the past, simply to move on? Or might that never be appropriate or even possible? I believe we must again tread a middle path where we can develop great awareness of all that we contain and all that we experience, even as we actively choose to create and experience something new. On one side of this very narrow middle path we run the risk of falling into using meditation only to relax, as a way of letting go of discomfort while failing ever to let go of its cause. In doing so we could condemn ourselves to an endless repetition of the cycle of pain and release, pain and release. On the other side of our middle way we face the possibility of using powerful techniques to forge ahead, to change our inner state without ever healing or releasing the old fears and patterns. On this side we run the risk of creating still another, albeit more subtle, form of denial.

The middle path I recommend takes us beyond simple awareness. By combining mindfulness with transformation practices, it gives us a blend of both peace and power. On the middle path we develop both a sensitively aware mind and the ability to choose, when appropriate, to let go and move on. On the middle path we shall make all of the psyche available to meditative examination, and we will free ourselves from old, unexamined limitations while we go ahead and create new mental and physical patterns. The combination will prove enormously effective. Specifically, this path uses stillness and mindfulness plus the kundalini yoga and meditation practices of breath control, posture, focus, mantra, affirmations, and visualization.

In ego we indulge ourselves, yet we hide from ourselves, from our old wounds, from the truth, and most especially from our own wisdom. In ego we don't know our true identity, and we may feel alienated, empty, and inauthentic. In ego we experience fear, anxiety, and negative aggressive states and find ourselves dominated by sexual desire and other appetites. We can't ignore these drives without the risk of fragmenting ourselves, of splitting into so-called acceptable and unacceptable parts. And yet indulging these fears and appetites never leads to lasting satisfaction. We cannot compensate for low self-esteem by catering to our inexhaustible appetites. Acting out of ego, we can never realize fulfillment.

On the middle path to peace we can recognize and honor all of this. Even as we do practices designed to take us beyond the ego, we will remain aware of its urges. The ego and the urges that have attached to it will not disappear through spiritual effort. Striving cannot get us past striving. We can, however, come to know the ego and through our meditation and yoga practices access our true self.

The pursuit of peace is our foundation, a first stage that we will never complete even as we proceed on to the subsequent stages of the success of the soul. We need to renew our peaceful-ness constantly, for each moment brings new challenges to our peaceful state of mind. We live in the midst of an unending stream of threats to peace. We experience desire and disappoint-ment, old age and decay, loss and death. We have our likes and dislikes, our senses of uncertainty and imperfection, our cares and ambitions. We ought to face our desires squarely, recogniz-ing, as egocentric beings, our extreme vulnerability to the effects of desire.

As children, no matter how well intentioned our parents may have been, we did not, could not, get enough approval and love to set us free of desire permanently. We have reacted by superimposing a coherence upon ourselves, a false persona that protects us from the effects of exploitation or lack of interest. We've become isolated within that false self and have created a fantasy of our own perfection: an unrealizable false self. We sac-rifice everything in pursuing it. We want nothing so much as the fulfillment of that ideal or, sometimes, just the appearance or the illusion of fulfillment.

For example, a girl who grows up without unconditional love and unlimited attention from her father might pursue end-lessly a fantasy of her perfect mate or might drive herself harshly at sports or work to get her father's approval. These psychological consequences have become well known and understood. But unfortunately we do not understand so well the possibility of peacefulness despite a lack of perfect love and complete fulfillment. The meditative way teaches us that we can transform our suffering into fascinating challenge. I do not suggest that we can live a life without difficulties. Rather I recognize that difficulties form an essential part of life that we can and must learn to work with.

We meditate for many reasons: relaxation, health, peace of mind, and so on. But honest meditative awareness leads to only one conclusion: We do not require less stress or more love or better health in order to find freedom and peace. Rather, our peace comes from a recognition that our soul welcomes these challenges. The soul knows, as our personal self hardly ever does, that these challenges are the classrooms of life.

In the end, all these words can do you very little good. Only the practice of meditation, sincere and devoted practice, can turn these intellectual ideas into something palpable and useful. If you intend to bring about an end to the suffering, to build a lasting peace founded on freedom from desire (rather than on a rickety foundation of temporarily satisfied desires), then begin now with your meditative practice.

Begin by establishing the time and place you will practice each day, as nothing can substitute for a daily practice, or *sadhana* (the time and effort devoted to spiritual work). Most people enjoy early-morning practice or a sadhana just before bed, but any time you can meditate undisturbed will serve you well.

Arrange your schedule so that you will feel free to practice then. If you need to rush to get out to work in the morning, you may have trouble relaxing into your meditation. Leave plenty of time to do your normal morning routine after you complete your meditation. If you meditate before bed, determine ahead of time when you will stop your other activities. You'll want to feel free to meditate. Help yourself by mentally affirming "The next ___ minutes are just for meditation. I set aside all else for now."

Ideally you will have some quiet room, a corner, someplace that you will set up for meditation with your cushion or mat, a pleasant, quiet decor, and perhaps an altar with some inspiring objects, books, or pictures. Don't think that you must have these things (just yesterday I meditated in a cab bouncing along the dusty road from Amritsar to Dharmasala, India), but all of it will help to set the mood and focus your mind.

I recommend a minimum of eleven minutes of meditation at one time, although you can certainly grab one-minute breaks during the day. It takes ten minutes for the body and mind to experience the effects of the meditation and to let go of tension; the eleventh minute is when you can connect with your un-limited self. More time usually feels better, although hours of just sitting without focus or stillness may have less value than a few minutes of full awareness. You may want to begin with an eleven-minute meditation in the early morning and another before bed, and then slowly increase the times up to half an hour or more. Commit to your daily minimum. Do it when you don't feel a need to meditate, and do it when you feel so depressed that you can hardly get out of bed. Just do it. Unless you are committed, it is very easy to find excuses not to meditate. Also make a commitment to do your sadhana for a minimum of forty days without a break. It will take that long to make meditation your habit.

Everyone will develop her own practice schedule and routine, but some guidelines might help. Try to do a morning sadhana, rising before the sun to meditate in the quietest time of day. If this seems too early for you, you might want to get up, do sadhana, then take a little nap before the business of your day begins. Whenever you do get up, stretch a little before getting out of bed. Then wash your hands, face, ears, neck, and feet with cold water (or really go for it and take a cold shower). This will stimulate your circulation and nervous system and wake you up. Brush your teeth and then your tongue, gagging a bit to clear out the impurities entrapped in the mucus of your throat during the night. Also sniff a little bit of water from the palm of your hand into your nostrils and blow your nose to further clean the mucous membranes. Although all of this may seem a bit strange, try it. Doing so will jump-start your body's engines and help to keep you healthy.

Then, dressed in loose, comfortable, and preferably natural-fiber clothing, tune in with the mantra "Ong Namo Guru Dev Namo" (as explained below and also in *Meditation for Absolutely Everyone*) and start your sadhana with breathing exercises and kundalini yoga. You will find the exercise sets I give in this and the next two chapters powerful and particularly well suited to our purposes. I recommend that you do one set of exercises for forty days before going on to the next set. During each forty-day period, also do that chapter's meditations and other suggested work. By the end of the forty days, you should have created positive new habits for peace, purpose, or prosperity.

The time for each exercise can vary (usually up to three minutes per exercise), so you can devote different amounts of time to your yoga according to your tastes and ability. On top of this try to do three minutes or more of breathing exercises and eleven minutes or more of meditation. Set aside enough time for all of this in one session, if possible. If this is all new to you, go easy on yourself. Do the exercises for a shorter time, or do the movements more slowly, until your capacity has increased.

After completing your yoga and before meditating, rest for a few minutes, relaxing deeply on your back, covered with a blanket. This will redistribute the energy awakened by the yoga and help quiet you for meditation. To end the relaxation, rub your palms together, rub the soles of your feet together (do yoga and meditate barefoot), pull your knees up to your chest and rock gently back and forth on your spine a few times. Then sit for your meditation in a comfortable posture using a mat or a pillow as necessary to create an erect, solid, steady posture with a straight spine. Cover your shoulders and back with a blanket or shawl.

You could do the mindfulness meditation you have already practiced with the tape. (Use the tape for as long as it seems helpful. At some point, you may prefer to go it alone.) However, a more effective practice would begin and end with a few minutes of mindfulness—as much as you would like—and in the middle, use one of the kundalini meditations to be described.

Yogi Bhajan taught these meditations, those I will give in the next chapters, and all the kundalini yoga sets. They combine awareness with body posture or movements, mantras, eye focus, breath control, and visualization. In the beginning you may find it difficult to keep track of all of this at once. Don't worry, many people have this feeling. Just begin your practice with whatever comes most easily—perhaps you will only do the movement and the breathing—and set aside, for now, whatever might be confusing you. Later it won't seem so daunting, and you'll easily do the complete practice.

Whereas simple mindfulness meditations give you a wonderful way to embrace all of the content of the mind and thus lead to the peacefulness of nonattachment, the kundalini techniques add to mindfulness ways to actually change the contents of the mind. With these techniques, mind and body can absorb thoughts, feelings, and attitudes consciously chosen to serve your spirit. During meditation you don't need to deny or suppress other thoughts, feelings, or attitudes; nevertheless, they will begin to fade out to the periphery of your consciousness while the meditation's message takes center stage.

TUNING IN

Yogi Bhajan has taught a method of preparation for sadhana that is particularly effective, although other ways may feel more comfortable for you. In his teaching we sit with our spine straight and bring our palms together with the thumbs pressed lightly against the center of the chest at the level of the heart. We then inhale deeply and slowly chant the sounds "Ong Namo Guru

Dev Namo" ("I bow to the Creator in all things. I bow to its divine wisdom"). Repeat this three to five times in a clear and powerful voice. This chant is demonstrated on Side 1 of the tape that comes with *Meditation for Absolutely Everyone.*

As an alternative way of tuning in, you might simply take three long, deep breaths as you mindfully come into the present. Or you can use a brief prayer or affirmation to establish that this time is for your awakening. Use whatever method seems best for you.

BREATHING EXERCISE 1: FOR A HEALTHY MENTAL BALANCE

For this breathing exercise, sit with your spine straight and inhale in twelve separate sniffs of air without any exhale between the inhales. By the time you have finished the twelfth part of the inhale, your lungs should feel completely full. You will then hold the breath in for as long as you can before exhaling in twelve parts and beginning again with another segmented inhale. Between the exhale and the next inhale you won't hold the breath out. Use your full lung capacity, expanding both abdomen and chest on the inhale and contracting chest and abdomen on the exhale. As you inhale, silently repeat the mantra "Sa Ta Na Ma" ("existence, life, death, rebirth"—explained in detail in *Meditation for Absolutely Everyone*) three times (one syllable per sniff), and do the same with the twelve-part exhale. Imagine the sound of three repetitions of "Sa Ta Na Ma" on the inhale and three more on the exhale. In the beginning, your lung capacity may make this twelve-part inhale and exhale a challenge. If it seems like too much, begin with a four-part or an eight-part breath. Later, as abdominal breathing becomes more natural and you become more used to long, deep breathing, you can go to the twelve-part breathing.

In this and in most of the techniques given in this book, you will have a fixed point of concentration for your eyes. We call this point the third eye, an imaginary spot about half an inch above the center of the eyebrows and half an inch inside the skull. To concentrate there, close your eyes, gently cross them, and roll them back, putting a slight pressure on the muscles that move the eyes. At first this may seem strange and could cause some slight discomfort in the eye muscles, but that sensation should not last for long.

Concentration at the third eye helps to focus and quiet the mind. If this seems like too much to do at first, when you are still getting used to the breathing pattern and the mantra, don't worry about it. Just do the exercise with your eyes closed in a relaxed, natural way. Later, when you feel ready, you can add in the third-eye focus. Use the concentration at the third eye in all the meditation and yoga in this book, except where otherwise noted.

Continue this breath pattern for as long as you would like to, up to a thirty-one-minute maximum. Start with a minimum of three minutes, then add one or two minutes each day. Do this anytime you have a few minutes and want to slow yourself down. Also do it for three minutes or more just before doing the yoga set given next or before meditation. It will help you to relax, quiet some of the mental chatter, and focus on the aim of peace.

I often do this, with eyes open, as I walk. Then I might do only a four-part inhale and exhale. Coordinate the breath with your stride and walk at a moderate to quick pace. I also have done this many times, in a quiet way, during meetings, counseling sessions, social gatherings, concerts or movies, or just about any time I want to maintain my mental balance and clarity.

KUNDALINI YOGA FOR PEACE

Once you have completed your breathing exercises, you can do the Kundalini Yoga Set for Peacefulness. This set specifically works on eliminating negative thought patterns and on balancing the function of the two hemispheres of the brain. It will also add to your radiance, energize you, and sensitize you to your own higher self. You can do each exercise for from one to three minutes. At the end, rest on your back to allow the new energy to balance and relax you deeply. Try to do this every day for forty days.

Warning: With this and the other yoga sets in this book, do not do anything that causes you pain. If you have any question as to whether you can safely do the yoga exercises suggested, consult your health care provider before beginning.

BREATH OF FIRE

Before giving you the specific exercises in this series, I'll teach you a few basic techniques that occur throughout kundalini yoga, as taught by Yogi Bhajan. In most of the exercises you will do what we call the "breath of fire." Breath of fire is very energizing. It serves to circulate a lot of air through the lungs in a short period of time. The blood is oxygenated, and carbon dioxide and pollutants are eliminated.

This breath uses the diaphragm and belly (as opposed to the rib cage and chest). To inhale, relax the muscles of the abdomen and expand the belly. The diaphragm, the large muscle that separates the thorax (chest) from the abdomen (belly), will drop and air will be drawn into your lungs. To exhale, pull the belly in rapidly. The diaphragm will raise and force air out. Breathe only through your nose. Imagine a candle in front of your nose and that your breath has enough force to blow it out as you exhale. Avoid breathing through your mouth or with your chest.

Practice this breath by placing one hand on your belly and one on your chest. As you do the breath, only your belly should move in and out. This will take a bit of practice. Have patience but strive to get it right. At first you may do this backward, pulling the belly in on the inhale and pushing it out on the exhale. Keep checking yourself to avoid this. Start slowly (one breath every few seconds). As you begin to master the breath pattern, pick up the speed. Eventually you'll be doing about one breath every second.

Breath of fire may not come easily for you. Some yoga students need quite a few classes before they are able to breathe abdominally. But abdominal breathing in general, and breath of fire in particular, will give you enormous benefits in return for the time you invest in mastering it.

You will also use mantras as you do the yoga. These words or sounds serve as a single thought to replace the many thoughts that usually clutter our minds. Most commonly we will use "Sat Nam" (rhymes with "but mom"), a mantra that refers to one's true identity, one's soul. Mentally, on the inhale repeat "Sat" and on the exhale repeat "Nam." If you know a short mantra from some other source, you may wish to use that instead. Just keep it in rhythm with your breath.

During the yoga you will also maintain your eye focus at the third eye as described earlier. All of these new techniques may seem confusing at first. If it feels like too much to think about in the beginning, start with just the physical posture or motion, with your eyes closed. When you feel comfortable with that, add in the breath of fire, then the focus at the third eye, and finally the mantra. After a little practice, all of these elements will blend together, and it will not seem difficult at all.

I am giving you only the fundamentals of kundalini yoga. There is a great deal more to learn than can be taught easily in a book. I suggest that you try to find a certified teacher near you. For the names and numbers of kundalini yoga teachers, call the International Kundalini Yoga Teachers Assoc. at 505-753-0423.

KUNDALINI YOGA SET FOR PEACEFULNESS

Exercise 1: Sit straight, with your arms to the side and raised up at a sixty-degree angle above the floor (see Figure 1). Keep your elbows straight. Have your palms facing up with the fingers pointing out to the sides. Begin a breath of fire and continue for one to three minutes. At first, do only what feels comfortable for you.

FIGURE 1

After you have been doing these yoga exercises for a while, you can increase the time up to the three-minute level. When you have completed the exercise, inhale deeply, suspend your breath for ten seconds or more, exhale and relax your hands down onto your lap. Sit still and relax deeply for one to three minutes before beginning the next exercise.

FIGURE 2   FIGURE 3

Exercise 2: Lie on your back. Bend your knees so that your heels are against your buttocks with the soles of your feet flat on the floor (Figure 2). Grab hold of your ankles. On the inhale, raise your hips up as high as you can (Figure 3). On the exhale, lower yourself back to the floor. Breathe with your abdomen. Do this slowly, at a rate of once in two or three seconds, for up to three minutes, according to your capacity. At the end, inhale, hold yourself in the up position, hold the breath in a relaxed way for ten seconds or more, and then relax down as you exhale. Stretch your legs out and relax on your back for one to three minutes.

FIGURE 4

Exercise 3: Put yourself into a triangle pose as shown in Figure 4. Begin a breath of fire starting with one minute and adding about fifteen seconds a day up to three minutes. Then take a deep breath in, suspend the breath for at least ten seconds, and come out of the posture. Sit or lie comfortably and relaxed for two minutes, concentrating at the third eye.

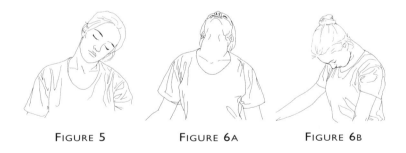

FIGURE 5   FIGURE 6A   FIGURE 6B

Exercise 4: Sitting straight, slowly and gently roll your head in circles around your neck (Figure 5). As with all exercise, avoid any pain. Let your breathing synchronize with the movement, one complete inhale and exhale for each revolution. After twelve revolutions, switch directions and do twelve more revolutions. Then rest for three minutes, focused at the third eye, and silently repeat your mantra ("Sat Nam" or any other one) with each breath. Then begin to inhale while gently stretching your neck backward (chin up) and exhale, stretching it forward (chin toward your chest) as shown in Figures 6a and 6b. Continue for up to three minutes.

Then deeply relax on your back before meditating. The audiotape included with *Meditation for Absolutely Everyone* includes a guided deep-relaxation sequence you may want to use at this time.

MEDITATION 2: A MEDITATION FOR PEACE (TAPE 2, SIDE 1)

The yoga and relaxation have prepared you for your meditation. Begin, if you wish, with a few minutes of quiet mindfulness. Then do eleven minutes or more of the following meditation. It will give you the ability to let go of your personal desires and to accept as gifts all that you have received, regardless of your personal preferences.

Sit, as always, with a straight spine. Use cushions as needed and imagine making yourself taller, lifting your chest and head, drawing in slightly on your chin and lengthening your spine. Do all of this in a relaxed way. Avoid rigidity. You may have to practice before you can sit in this dignified posture without becoming fatigued, but make the effort. Sitting will become easier over time.

FIGURE 7

Hold your hands as if you were going to catch water in them. Bring the sides of the palms and the little fingers together with the palms up, forming a little cup at the level of your heart. Hold this hand posture in a relaxed way, with the fingers slightly bent. Refer to Figure 7.

As you do the meditation, chant this mantra:

Ek Ong Kar
Sat Gur Prasaad
Sat Gur Prasaad
Ek Ong Kar

This may be roughly translated as "There is only one consciousness, throughout all of creation. This truth is known by grace. By grace we know this truth and are able to experience this one consciousness." Contemplate the meaning of God as the All in all. That oneness, all of creation, comes as a gift of the Divine. Once we recognize this fact, then which of our troubles shall we reject? Which difficult person should we shun? If all comes by God's grace, what judgment could we possibly pass? This mantra is sacred and powerful. Use it with reverence.

To chant this mantra, inhale and slowly repeat the entire mantra as you exhale. Keep up a steady rhythm for eleven minutes or more (up to sixty-two minutes). Practice chanting this way a few times before you add the next step.

When you have become familiar with the mantra, you can significantly increase the effectiveness of this meditation by rhythmically pumping your diaphragm as you chant. Pull in on the navel area muscles, contracting the belly and lifting the diaphragm each time you chant "Ek Ong" and release as you chant "Kar." Also pump in as you chant "Sat Gur" and release on "Prasaad" so that for each repetition of the mantra, you complete four contractions and four releases. This will create waves of tension and relaxation, over and over. You may feel a good deal of heat in your body as you do this advanced yoga technique, and you may find it to be too much at first. If so, simply do the meditation without pumping your diaphragm. Later, when you feel able, you can add in the pumping, beginning very gently. A teacher of kundalini yoga will be able to help you with this.

When you have done the meditation for the allotted time, take a deep breath in, suspend your breath—holding it without any strain—for ten seconds or so, and then relax the breath. Sit still, meditating mindfully for as long as you wish. During this time let only the most positive thoughts into your mind and picture yourself and others as healthy, happy, and holy. Before getting up, stretch your arms high into the air and shake your hands vigorously for a few seconds to bring you back into an alert, grounded consciousness.

This meditation has the power to take you beyond your egocentric desires. It lets you relax with the gifts that the universe gives you instead of fighting for what you think you should have and running from what you don't want. Often we have difficulty understanding the wisdom of what comes to us. Only slowly may we come to understand the hidden lessons and blessings in an apparent catastrophe. A great soul maintains an attitude of gratitude, even in the face of difficult times. We all need to cultivate precisely this humility and awareness if we wish to live peacefully.

Again, I recommend doing this meditation along with the kundalini yoga and breathing exercises given in this chapter. Do this routine every day. Keep at your practice for forty days straight while remaining conscious of the principles of peacefulness discussed in this chapter. This effort will help you to make peace your habit.

I hope that you will use the techniques given here in a conscientious manner. Peace in the world begins as peace of mind. Whenever we choose to remain peaceful in the face of challenge, we change the world. I see peace as our right as human beings and also our responsibility. Please take this to heart and do your part to heal your world.

4
PURPOSE

Do you know what you have come here to do, what you might do in your lifetime that will bring you the greatest satisfaction and sure knowledge that you have used your self and this time well? Do you know the way that you can do the most for the world around you, the way that you can serve and take real joy in that service? Few people ever ask themselves such questions, and many fewer ever get satisfying answers, answers that they can work with as they organize their lives. Most who do ask will get only a simple answer. They will conclude that they should live long and well, raise a family in a loving way, give back some of what they have received, and provide for the future.

But such a vision of life's purpose does not go far enough. It doesn't provide specifics of what we might do. What exactly does it mean to live well, to love, to give or serve, or to provide for the future? This vision, while filled with the best of intentions, does not contain enough rich detail to guide our actions.

We need a highly personalized vision, a soulful vision that puts us in touch with our deepest yearnings. We need to know, with our whole being, the highest function that we might serve, and we need to know this in a way that can guide our everyday actions. When you reach such clarity of purpose, making decisions about career, spiritual practice, community activities, political action, and even recreation becomes much easier. When you have clear purpose, you know how to manage your time. You have enthusiasm for the tasks that you need to accomplish and more easily eliminate the extraneous from your life. With a sense of purpose, one frees oneself from association with negative people or other harmful influences. And with purpose comes greater understanding as to how to act in any given situation. When you know your destination, you can make intelligent choices about how to get there.

In this chapter we will go into the process of seeking such clear vision, and we will examine some of the characteristics of vision. In seeking vision, we now embark on one of the great adventures of a spiritual life. I hope that you will give this great adventure all the energy and effort required. We live in an exciting time in the history of humankind, a time of greater and more rapid change than at any other time. As the world changes, individuals change, relationships change, economics and politics change. In a time such as this, we have an enormous need for leadership on all levels of society. In families, in religious congregations, in government, in business, in every other human grouping, we need leaders who can provide direction based on consciousness and vision.

We are experiencing a good deal of confusion in the world and can expect that the confusion will only increase in the years ahead. The old ways do not work as they once did, and new paths must be blazed. Hierarchical and patriarchal models of culture have had their day, but they will not give way passively to more egalitarian models. Wholesale destruction of our habitat and our communities at the hands of profit-motivated multinational corporations must stop, but it will not stop spontaneously. The trends toward urban decay and the descent of millions into poverty while the richest among us get still richer must reverse, but they will not reverse on their own. We need a veritable revolution, a turning from fear, greed, and exploitation to a new ethic of kindness and sharing, an ethic based on elevated consciousness. Such a revolution can occur. It can start within each and every aware individual. By seeking vision based on a foundation of peacefulness, we can come to understand our true roles as leaders in the evolution of humankind.

What shifts should happen in your life? How will you best position yourself to contribute to the betterment of yourself and others? Among your friends and acquaintances you must know a few who have given up one way of life for another more compelling one, who at some point simply knew that they had to make fundamental changes. Perhaps you too have felt or will feel this need. Or perhaps more subtle changes may take place. You may need to make a deeper commitment to some elements of your current lifestyle or let go of some of the old patterns of behavior that have dominated you for so long.

These questions have no right or wrong answers, of course, only *your* answers. Some people will learn that they must raise themselves to become teachers to thousands; others may learn that they need to love more unconditionally, to slow down and appreciate life more, to quietly serve as an example to a few. To know what your soul calls for will require looking deeply within yourself. The answers may not come easily.

How do we do cultivate our vision? First of all, before all else, we need to keep up in our meditative practices, to remain clear and peaceful even as we go further and ask for greater insight. Without this foundation we can have little hope for real understanding. If you have not yet begun to devote some of each day to this spiritual work, begin now. You will find no substitute for the daily reuniting of your personal self to your soul.

You do not need to somehow perfect this meditation practice or this yoga, this union, before we can move on. You merely need to bring the intention of unity into daily life, allowing yourself to let go of difficult inner states and allowing peace and love to grow in you instead. This will not happen spontaneously. It takes the effort of facing yourself and a willingness to allow yourself to be transformed.

If we wish to see our world transformed, we will need to start with the intention of transforming ourselves. No matter how insignificant our place, no matter how small the world we inhabit, if we radically change ourselves, then perhaps we can change the world at large. Within the smaller action of individual change lies hidden the larger action of collective change.

Individual change comes from within. If you deliberately try to change yourself to conform to some outer ethic, with some newer, better propaganda, then no real changes will result, only a superficial rearrangement of your characteristics. Real change results when we honestly explore the territory of the unknown. If we only enter the realm of the known, with our success guaranteed because we have traveled there before, then we limit ourselves to superficial change. Real change, revolution in consciousness, happens only when we are willing to go where we have no prior experience and to look squarely at whatever we may find.

Once you have gained some confidence in your meditation, once you have begun to observe, without flinching, the contents of your mind and body, then the time to seek a vision of the purpose of your soul has arrived. While I cannot suggest what your vision might contain, I can safely say a little about the kind of vision that you will seek.

Think of yourself as a soul inhabiting a human body and mind. This body/mind complex has taken on great importance to you, and you identify with it so much that you call it "me." You measure your success in terms of the comfort you've provided to the body/mind, and now you wish to bring a greater spiritual awareness into the body/mind as a way of advancing yourself and your comfort level still further. You may believe that by progressing spiritually, you will sooner or later reach a state of bliss, the ultimate success of life. Thus you may have set goals based on comfort, illumination, and bliss, and your life plan, if you have one, will be a plan to serve the body/mind in ways that will lead you toward these goals. You will try to bring more soul into your life. In this way you will use soulfulness as a way of serving the needs of the personality, of the body/mind.

This approach can lead to relief of much of the grosser sorts of discomfort. But while it can give some symptomatic relief, it cannot heal the fundamental disease of desire. Desire, and the suffering that our desire engenders, springs from our fears and our perceived need to ensure the survival of the body/mind. No program, no purpose, that aims only at the comfort of the body/mind can possibly get beyond all this. We will need to turn this entire approach upside down before we can possibly receive genuinely new vision.

Instead of asking how the soul might serve the needs of the personality, we need to ask how the personality might serve the soul. This radically different question leads to radically different answers, answers that will take us where we must go. When we go back to the fundamental assumption that the soul inhabits and uses this body/mind for its own purposes, then the question of purpose takes on a whole new meaning.

A sense of purpose derived from this assumption will have certain characteristics. It will provide inspiration as to how you might transform yourself, it will enable you to understand how to manage the details of life, and it will tell you of your highest function. This vision will bring you a sense of destiny. It will endure, evolving slowly if at all during the course of your life. It will prove intensely personal, perhaps never spoken of. It will have rich meaning and subtle detail that might take a long time to fully understand. It may come in symbols not easily understood. At first it may not seem confluent with your personality, but through the fulfillment of your vision, your life will become soulful and filled with unimagined riches and joy. Fulfillment of your vision also may subject you to trials of mythic proportions.

Meditation shall form the basis for your seeking of this vision. You will use awareness and a heightened sensitivity to your own inner states as the major tools of the vision quest. These are the skills you are honing through the practices taught in the previous chapter. Other than meditation, each of us will select other tools to use according to our own instincts. In the pages that follow, and on the tape that comes with this book, I present a variety of possible ways to open your consciousness to vision. Experiment with all of them. Use them over and over as you see fit.

Allow your vision to come to you all at once in a flash or in many small pieces. Allow it to evolve and change over time if it must. But beware of your personality's tricky way of modifying your soul's vision, of diluting it, of compromising its core values. The personality has its own agenda and its own much more limited vision, and it may try to subvert the vision of the soul. Perhaps the most common lament I hear from my students is how, despite their inspiration and best intentions to keep up their spiritual practice, there is always some other priority, or too little time, or too much laziness. This is their personality drawing them away from the vision of their souls. In other cases, heartfelt, lifelong urges to paint or become a physician or own a restaurant are neglected and eventually forgotten, replaced by more primitive urges for, as an example, safety and security. Again, the personality tends to pull back from the soul's inspiration. The most important thing you can do is to respect your vision, honor its wisdom, and follow its direction, come what may. Despite the inertia or fears of your personality, keep relating to the truth of who you are, of who you might become.

A woman I had counseled for several months continued to tell me that she was ready to give up her promiscuity, her smoking, and her drugs. She had surrounded herself with sweet pictures, inspiring mottoes, and all sorts of supposedly uplifting paraphernalia. All that was missing was a real vision, a real connection to the call of her soul. She had only a desire to be happy but no plan and no real sense of what that happiness might look like. When I began to probe this area, encouraging her to look at her future self, she resisted. After she phoned several times when she was under the influence of cocaine, calls that I clearly told her were not welcome, she terminated our counseling relationship. This woman let the weaknesses of her personality rule; clearly, her life—and ours—would be better regulated by the soul. What we all require to achieve this is both vision and a genuine commitment to that vision.

In our culture we do not have a tradition of the vision quest, but we ought to. We need to invent new ways to acquire vision that are appropriate to our times. To help with that, let us look at a traditional way of searching for insight. In many of the cultures native to the Americas, the vision quest was a formal event in the life of young people as they prepared to take their place as adults in society.

The vision quest often began with a sweat lodge ceremony in which the body and mind underwent a symbolic and physical cleansing. The sweat lodge tested the participants. At times, the heat could seem unbearable, and without calmness one's fears would only intensify the discomfort. The sweat lodge was a spiritual ceremony as well as a method of purification, of healing, of becoming whole. When used at the beginning of a vision quest, it prepared a person for what was to come, emptying the mind of fear, self-doubt, judgment, analysis, and expectations. Following the sweat, the quester typically would go off alone for days of fasting and meditation, perhaps naked except for a blanket.

Native Americans understood that humans could never grasp the spirit world through words or concepts or logical thought. The quester needed to set all that aside, to feel with heart and perceive with a pure mind. The world of spirit could not be explained; it could only be experienced. Visions of that world often came in nuance and almost imperceptible communications. To aid in receiving these communications, the site of the vision quest was chosen carefully: separate from the activities of society, restful, but not a place of grand vistas or other dramatic scenery. The ideal location provided little for the mind to feed on.

Fasting enhanced receptivity. The vision quester went as an empty vessel, as if he or she had neither past nor future. Into this vessel, it was hoped, came the vision, either all at once, magnificently complete, or in smaller bits and pieces, over a period of time and many quests.

After the vision quest, the real tests began, for the one with vision had to honor that vision in everyday life. Having gained insight and wisdom, she then had the challenge of bringing that wisdom into society, of using it for the common good. Having communicated with the world of spirit, the quester had to maintain awareness of spirit even as she functioned in the world of humans.

In our day, in contemporary society, few of us will duplicate the Native American vision quest (although I have actually seen advertisements for expensive vision quest package tours). Nevertheless, we can learn a great deal from this tradition, from its essential elements. In the old way, the one who sought vision purified himself, removed himself from the everyday world, eliminated distractions, meditated, fasted, remained as open and receptive as possible, was grateful for any wisdom received, and subsequently struggled to maintain the purity of the vision and its teachings as he brought them back into everyday life. We will do exactly this, in our own way.

Do you feel ready to embark on this adventure of seeking vision? I suggest that you ask this question of yourself in a serious way. You will, first of all, need to hold yourself in reasonable stillness. Above all else, you will devote this time to listening, to tuning in to that which we normally don't perceive. You'll also need to open yourself to the possibility of surprising answers to your questions about purpose. If you go into this process expecting certain kinds of answers, you diminish your chances of hearing subtle voices pointing in new, unexpected directions. Expectation precludes vision.

On the other hand, you will want to cultivate your sense of expectancy, the belief that something wonderful could happen at any time. This means holding your mind in a state of suspension: quiet, broadly alert, open, still, and neutral. With this sense of expectancy you will let go of all desire (including even the desire for understanding of purpose). When you cultivate this state, you cannot predict what will happen. When I have done formal vision quests, I have gotten all sorts of input, some of it very related to my overall life purpose but some of it what I would call detail: clarity about what piece of land to buy, a single word ("listening") that gave new focus to my meditation, once even an idea for the design of a sailboat. Had I gone into these situations with expectations instead of expectancy, I might not have "heard" these details, all of which have become very important to me.

If you do feel ready to hold to a stillness and an attitude of expectancy, think through how you will approach your vision quest. Although you may not get out into the wilderness for three or four days of fasting and meditation, you should arrange to separate yourself from your normal life and its set routines for a time. That time could last an hour, an afternoon, days, or even weeks. Step out of the normal and into a time and space both peaceful and different. Borrow a friend's cottage for a weekend, take off a day from work in the middle of the week, or schedule a completely undisturbed hour for yourself. Anyone can do this, although it always saddens me when I hear people tell me that they don't think that they could possibly get some quiet time to themselves. I don't think that they really want it. Once you have determined that you can, and will, get off by yourself, get the cooperation of your friends, family, and others in your life who might unwittingly disturb you if they didn't understand your intention.

If you feel that you can get only an hour or two, you will do well to plan a number of these miniretreats. Even if you can get off for days at a time, you might very well repeat this every six months or so, as I do. Don't get so caught up in the demands of everyday life that you forget your higher self.

Having decided how much time you feel comfortable giving to yourself in this way, next consider cleansing. If you have never fasted, I would not suggest that you go off by yourself for three days without any food. But before and during the time of your retreat, eat as lightly as you can. Avoid hard-to-digest foods and those that make you feel stuffed. Eat little and you will meditate more easily. Make yourself into an empty vessel, literally and figuratively, and you will create some room in which to receive.

In addition to dietary cleansing, clean yourself of stimulants, alcohol, recreational drugs, tobacco, and so on. These substances do nothing positive; they only rob you of clarity. Also, clean your outer body. Take a shower or bath, ending with stimulating cold water. Clean your environment. Turn off the phone and loud, disruptive music. Create a neat and clean area for your retreat. Eliminate as much of the external stimuli as possible, replacing it with sights and sounds that soothe you. If you are not sure whether something should come with you on your retreat, eliminate it. Less is more. You may want one or two inspiring books or pictures, but in general you'll look inward, at your own inspiration, and not to the creations of others.

Having done all this outer preparation, again pay attention to your inner, mental preparation. Going into the vision time, tune in and sit silently for a time. Then begin talking gently to yourself or praying in your own way. Focus on your intent, on emptying yourself so that you may learn. Ask for whatever stillness, commitment, perseverance, humility, devotion, or other qualities you feel you will need in order to complete the vision quest. Affirm your readiness, willingness, and ability to go through the time ahead and that you will make every effort to heed whatever guidance you may receive.

If your session will last for a long time, if you will go off on an extended retreat, you will not only meditate but probably will alternate yoga, breathing exercises, meditations, contemplation, and mental exercises. You'll also devote some of your time to your personal toilet, simple meals, housekeeping, and perhaps writing in a journal. On the shortest retreats, when you have only an hour or two, or a half day, you'll restrict yourself to a few of these elements, such as breath, yoga, meditation, and mental exercises.

You also might consider the possibility of temporarily adopting a semimonastic lifestyle. In the first months after I retired from my practice of dentistry, I experimented with this approach as I consciously went about redesigning my life. I did not want to busy myself with activities that filled my time and amused me. I wanted what I did to help me define a more meaningful way of living in the world. I devoted much more time to meditation and yoga and tried to approach each task as meditation, as a further opportunity for awareness. I avoided, as much as I could, the usual busyness. Whenever I noticed that I was rushing or not paying attention to what I was doing, I would stop and do whatever meditation was necessary—a minute or an hour—to bring myself back to center. More recently, as I have taken on more activities, I have tried to maintain some of this retreat mentality, and it has served me well. I am better able than before to choose wisely from among the infinite variety of possible activities, and I am less willing than before to get caught up in anything that doesn't serve the purposes of my soul.

For your use, in whatever way you give attention to the vision process, I offer you here some breathing exercises, kundalini yoga, and meditations. They will help open you to vision. On Tape 1 that comes with this book, I take you through two different guided meditations, experiences that should help you to imagine still more of your potential.

BREATHING EXERCISES FOR PURPOSE

Use these breathing techniques by themselves or before yoga or meditation. You can do them for any length of time that you wish. Start with no more than eleven minutes and build your time up slowly, adding just two or three minutes a day. Most people should do no more than thirty-one or sixty-two minutes. Tune in (with "Ong Namo Guru Dev Namo") before beginning each session.

BREATHING EXERCISE 2:
PREPARATION FOR YOGA OR MEDITATION

This exercise will help develop in you two very important qualities. The first, humility, frees you from unreasonable attachment to your personal agenda and helps you to surrender to the agenda of your soul. The second quality, gratitude, allows you to accept whatever you have received, with equal gratitude for the pleasant and the painful. These qualities do not add up to blind acceptance of fate or to giving up your efforts to fulfill your personal preferences. Rather, humility and gratitude allow you to work with what is. They free you from some of the pain of disappointment. They enable you to find the opportunities in difficult circumstances. They help to get you off of the emotional roller coaster. Humility and gratitude are two of the keys to unlock your soulfulness. In this breathing exercise, hold onto an awareness of both humility and thankfulness as you go through the process.

You will breathe through alternate nostrils. Begin by using the right thumb to block off the right nostril and take a deep abdominal inhale through the left nostril to a count of four (or, if you wish, one repetition of the mantra "Sa Ta Na Ma"). Then use thumb and ring finger to block off both nostrils while you hold the breath in for a count of sixteen (or four repetitions of "Sa Ta Na Ma"). Next you will exhale through the right nostril while holding the left nostril closed with the ring finger. Exhale to a count of eight (or two repetitions of "Sa Ta Na Ma").

Take the next inhale, begun as soon as you have finished the exhale, through the right nostril. After holding the breath, you will exhale through the left nostril. The third inhale will again come through the left nostril, and so on. Slowing the breath down as much as possible will benefit you. Begin with whatever you find comfortable and gradually increase the time for each breath, aiming for one breath per minute but not expecting that to come easily. Even at rates of two, three, or four breaths per minute you will get tremendous benefit. If you wish, as your breathing rate slows down, you can double the number of repetitions of the mantra. Just keep the 1:4:2 ratio of the inhale, hold, and exhale. As with all the techniques in this book, you can profitably do this as a forty-day sadhana. Do it for eleven to thirty-one minutes, building up your time a little each day.

This is a complex breathing pattern, and performing it will require you to be clearly focused. Like many of the techniques in this book, you may have to practice before you are comfortable with it. Start slowly. Do a few minutes, rest, and then do a little more. Check and double check the instructions. Be sure you are using your diaphragm and abdomen as you breathe. Don't worry; a little bit of dedicated practice will get you through the difficulties.

KUNDALINI YOGA FOR PURPOSE

Here I give you a more challenging yoga set that will serve you as you go through the vision process. It is designed to open up your intuitive capacities so that you will be better able to understand your own path. Hold the exercises for whatever length of time works for you. Do what you can at first, and build up your stamina over time. Keep up and make whatever progress you can. If a particular exercise seems too challenging for you or if for some reason you feel you shouldn't do it, try doing it mentally.

Imagine your body in the position, or get as close to the position as you can and go ahead and do the breathing and concentration for the prescribed time. This will give you more of the benefits than you might expect.

With yoga, as with any physical discipline, avoid pain. However, push yourself a bit, exploring your limits, finding out what it feels like if you stretch a bit more or keep up for five more seconds. Find a balance between shying away from any difficulty or discomfort, on the one hand, and taking a macho, no-pain, no-gain approach on the other. Aim for gradual improvement in your strength, flexibility, and endurance. Let the improvements come not so much from driving yourself to greater heights of performance but from relaxing tension, depending more on the breathing, deepening concentration, and the like. To benefit from yoga, you do not have to be extremely strong or flexible. Quite the contrary. Most of the benefits of doing these exercises come from simply experiencing yourself as you are, without judgment, as you do what you can. Find your own balance in all this. Eventually this approach will give you the results you really want: peace, purpose, and prosperity. Have fun with the yoga and it will give you back a great deal.

Kundalini Yoga Set for Purpose

Exercise 1: Back Platform Pose. Face upward, legs outstretched, and lean back on your hands. Inhale and lift yourself up onto just your hands and feet, to a position in which your body forms a straight line (see Figure 8). Exhale as you lower your buttocks to

FIGURE 8   FIGURE 9

the floor as shown in Figure 9. Breathe deeply with your abdomen. Mentally use the mantra "Sat Nam" (inhale "Sat," exhale
"Nam") as you continue to go up and down at a rate of about
once in five seconds. Keep up for from one to five minutes. As
always, work to your own capacity. If you need to start with just
one repetition of the movement, that is fine. Just do it with
awareness, allowing yourself to be just as you are. Concentrate at
the third eye. Do this and all yoga as an inner experience. At the
end inhale deeply, hold briefly in the up position, and then exhale
and relax down, lying on your back for about three minutes.

FIGURE 10

Exercise 2: Modified Bow Pose. Lying on your stomach, reach
back and take hold of your ankles and then pull your ankles
toward your head, arching into a bow, keeping your chin on the

ground (Figure 10). Begin a breath of fire, remembering the mantra, and concentrating at the third eye. Keep up for as much as three minutes. At the end, inhale, hold the breath for ten seconds, and then completely relax, allowing your breath to return to normal, and turn your head to one side. After a minute repeat the same exercise, but hold onto your big toes instead of your ankles. Do this for one minute and then relax completely.

FIGURE 11

Exercise 3: Maha Mudra (the Great Gesture). Sit on your left heel with your right leg straight out in front of you. Reach down and hold your right big toe with your right hand, squeezing the center of the toe between index finger and thumb. Hold the right heel with your left hand. Keep your eyes open and stare, without blinking, at your right big toe (Figure 11). Breathe like you would if you were doing a very slow breath of fire. Breathe with your abdomen but at a rate of one breath in five to ten seconds, mentally repeating "Sat Nam" as you go. On the exhale, imagine energy rising up your spine and projecting out your eyes. Keep this up for from one to fifteen minutes. Then reverse the posture so that the left leg goes out, and repeat. At the end, sit and relax meditatively.

There are many aspects to Maha Mudra: breath, concentration, posture, imagining the energy rising, mantra. At first this may feel overwhelming. If it does, simply do what you can. Begin with the posture, then add the eye focus. After some practice, add in the breathing pattern and mantra. Finally, work with the feeling of energy rising. Each step in this will take you further.

As for the posture itself, it may be beyond your current flexibility. If so, you might begin with reaching toward your toe, rather than trying to hold it with thumb and forefinger. Keep relaxing the tense areas and over time you will see progress. An alternative would be to bend your knee in order to reach your toe. If this proves necessary, relax into the stretch with the intention of going a bit farther each day.

Sitting on your heel may also challenge you. If so, try beginning with brief periods and then switching to a position with your heel tucked up against your groin. If your knee winds up high off the floor, slowly work at stretching it down. Again, use relaxation of the tense areas rather than force to gain in flexibility.

FIGURE 12

Exercise 4: Sit in any comfortable posture, raise your arms over your head, stretching up with your elbows straight (Figure 12).

Put your palms together, but allow a little space between the centers of the palms. Concentrate at the third eye. Breathe normally and meditate on your breath while mentally repeating your mantra. Keep up for one to three minutes.

This entire yoga set works on increasing your intuition. This will help as you ponder your purpose.

MEDITATIONS FOR PURPOSE

In general, do a set of yoga exercises before doing a meditation. This will give you energy and focus and help make the meditation more effective. However, you can do these meditations by themselves if you need to. Eleven minutes is a good minimum time for meditation, but the goal might be to work up to thirty-one minutes or more. Once you have reached the duration you want to work at, aim for forty days at that level without missing even one day. A forty-day sadhana will change old patterns and help you to create powerful new habits.

MEDITATION 3: FOR EMOTIONAL CLARITY (TAPE 2, SIDE 2)

This meditation will bring you new clarity of thought, unaffected by emotions. It will enable you to make wiser choices and set more meaningful directions for your life, without interference from your inner, personal states, such as fear, guilt, or even excitement. With this meditation something radical just might occur: a revolution in consciousness.

We cannot just rearrange the elements of our lives in order to find the happiness we desire. That will not do the trick. No amount of trying harder or bringing more control to bear on our difficulties or doing more of one thing and less of another will set us free. This approach will lead only to temporary improvements and give us a false sense of progress. When we strive in this way, when we make sacrifices so as to get everything done or to be a better person, we delude ourselves. We simply cannot go far enough that way.

It is as if we have been struggling up a steep hill in order to reach a reward on the top. We've made great effort, overcome all sorts of obstacles, and exhausted ourselves in the struggle for the reward. We've finally gotten to the top and see now that the reward is suspended above the ground just out of reach. No amount of struggle of the kind that we have already engaged in will enable us to reach our goal. A new kind of effort will be required.

All of us have struggled long and hard for various rewards. But now we must face the fact that everything we have done up until now has just served to prepare us. Now, if we wish to achieve our real goals, we must do something entirely different. For our whole lives we have learned that struggle will make us happy. Now we see that struggle, at best, can put us on top. Happiness, our real goal, can come to us only when we stop struggling.

This particular meditation will take what you have always struggled with, namely your suppressed or hidden emotions or negative emotions that you have too readily acted out, and establish a new, collaborative relationship with them. It will convert the beast within into a helper, eliminating the struggle among the various aspects of your personality and enabling you to emerge as a unified force, moving along in a coherent way. The beast will become the power and passion in you as you move to a new level of understanding.

In order to move forward in consciousness, to get out of the struggle for the top and make the leap required to secure happiness, we must understand purpose. But the underside of the subconscious mind clouds this understanding with emotions that block vision. Thus, most of us never come to understand what we really want. In this meditation, the shadowy underside of consciousness is brought into the light and its energy is coordinated with the energy of the soul, helping you to achieve clarity of purpose.

FIGURE 13

As always, sit straight and tune in. For this meditation, your eyes will be just one-tenth open in a soft focus. Interlock your fingers with the fingers inside the palms, pointing toward you. Do this with the right index finger uppermost on the stack of fingers and the left little finger on the bottom of the stack. Then take the right middle finger out of its position and lay it on the back of your left hand. Finally, to complete this complex hand posture, press the tips of the thumbs together so that they point up, and rest your hands against the upper part of your belly, at the level of the diaphragm as shown in Figure 13.

This meditation will involve chanting the mantra

So Hung Har Har Har Har So Hung

"*So Hung*" indicates an identity between you and "*Har*," the Creator. We have available to us literally millions of mantras in many different languages. This one, and others in this book, come from Gurmukhi, the sacred language of the Sikhs, but their universal meanings don't pertain to any one religion or spiritual path.

In chanting this mantra, use a monotone and separate the syllables so as to create eight separate beats. The sound "Har" will be pronounced with the tongue striking the palate on the *r*. This is the same tongue position as in the *d* in the word "bud."

Take only one breath for each repetition of the mantra, which should last about eight seconds, and use up all of your breath. The inhale between repetitions will take another four or five seconds. This speed (about four repetitions per minute) will slow down your breathing and calm your mind.

Do the entire meditation with your navel point pulled in, relaxing it only as you inhale. This will provide a significant boost to the power of the meditation and help to bring about the transformation from emotion-centered to soul-centered vision. Pulling the navel in helps to take energy normally devoted to our basic animal needs (food, warmth, sex, etc.) and direct it toward our higher human functions (love, compassion, intuition, speaking the truth, and so on).

Practice for eleven minutes at first. As you become comfortable with the meditation, gradually extend your time up to thirty-one minutes each day. When you have completed the formal meditation, just sit quietly. In the stillness of this moment, which you can extend for as long as you wish, ask for guidance. Open yourself. Hold yourself in a sense of expectancy, and listen. Work with this meditation over a period of time, forty days or more. During the same period, do the yoga and breathing exercises given earlier in this chapter and you will be well on your way to a new and deeper understanding of purpose.

MEDITATION 4:
A BREATH MEDITATION FOR INTUITION

This simple, silent meditation will help you to know what has always seemed unknowable. It will open your receptivity to subtle information, those ideas and impulses that you might have previously missed or ignored. Therefore, this meditation will prepare you for vision. It can be practiced for any length of time from three to five minutes (for a quick refocus in the middle of the day) up to thirty-one minutes (as a part of your morning or evening sadhana).

Begin, as usual, by tuning in and sitting with a straight spine. Hold your right hand at shoulder level with the palm facing forward. Extend the index and middle fingers straight up and hold the fourth (ring) and fifth (pinkie) fingers with the thumb, as if you were giving the peace symbol. Hold your left hand at the center of your chest with your arm parallel to the ground and the palm facing down. Extend all your fingers straight.

Concentrate your vision by focusing at the third eye, closing your eyes, gently crossing them and rolling them back as if you wanted to gaze at the inside of the center of your brow. This way of focusing your eyes helps to quiet and focus the mind. Also, according to the yogic understanding of the body's subtle anatomy and physiology, it will directly stimulate the pituitary gland, considered important to intuition.

Now, begin to breathe very slowly and deeply. Normally, we tend to breathe in a limited way, using only the chest, expanding and contracting the rib cage. A more natural breath begins with abdominal breathing in which the belly relaxes and expands so as to let the diaphragm drop. When this happens, the chest cavity enlarges, drawing air into the lungs. Then the rib cage expands to further enlarge the chest cavity and bring in still more air. For complete exhales, first the rib cage contracts and then the belly pulls in, pushing out the last bit of air. This may sound complex, but it will take no conscious thought once you have become used to it. As a young child you breathed this way. People trained as singers, musicians, martial artists, or athletes all learn to breathe abdominally. Take some time to understand these instructions and to practice abdominal breathing, not just for this meditation but for general good health and vitality.

In this particular meditation, you should breathe as slowly as possible. In the beginning this may mean five or six breaths per minute, but work at reducing the rate of breathing more and more, with a goal of only one breath per minute. This will probably challenge you, but don't worry. Just keep up at the practice and you'll make progress over time. As you do you will notice your mental processes become more relaxed and peaceful and your intuitive mind will awaken. To take this to a point of extreme effectiveness, try to breathe one breath per minute, thirty-one minutes per day, for forty days without missing a day.

You can repeat this forty-day sadhana whenever you want, any time that you feel your intuition needs a boost. You also can use the hand position and breath pattern for brief periods throughout the day, whenever you feel the need. Once you have worked with this for a while, just three minutes will effectively tune up your intuition.

GUIDED MEDITATIONS FOR PURPOSE
(TAPE 1, SIDES 1 AND 2)

The guided meditations on the tape will help you to see yourself in a new light and to imagine a future elevated and fruitful. In order to use these meditations to the best advantage, try to do them when you have the time to precede them with some of the yoga, breath control, and meditations given in this chapter. No special instructions are needed for these meditations. Simply relax, turn on the tape, and let it guide you.

In doing the first of these two guided meditations, you will need to stop the tape several times to write down your thoughts, so prepare yourself with paper and pen. You will go through the entire second meditation before doing any writing. I suggest that you begin now to keep a notebook or journal devoted to what you learn as you go through the vision process. I keep my own journal in a small blank book in which I make occasional entries, whenever I get some new insight.

When we clear away the confusion of day-to-day life, put ourselves into a meditative mind, and then ask for guidance, that guidance will come. Go into the guided meditations with an attitude of careful listening, first to the meditation itself and then, more important, to your own inner voices. Before turning on the tape, affirm that you seek clarity and honesty and that you expect insight. Out of these exercises, and the other meditations and exercises, will come new images, new voices, and a new intensification of your subtle intelligence. Affirm your readiness to listen to whatever messages you may receive and your willingness to honor them, taking on the tasks of your soul.

You will need to decide for yourself how to best approach the vision process. It might work best if you devote a little time each day to vision, a few minutes perhaps, at the end of your sadhana. Or you might set aside an hour for this work once each week. You may prefer an extended vision quest of several days in a remote location. I use all of these approaches.

Consciously cultivate your ability to tap into a higher source of wisdom, as if a wise teacher were speaking within you. To hear the teacher's wisdom, you need only quiet yourself and listen. For some of us, quieting our minds that much takes some dedication; nevertheless, when we make the effort, the voice of wisdom comes through.

In all this we must recognize that our wisdom and understanding may have become limited, over time, by our personality, culture, and life experiences. If we care to understand the purposes of our souls, we'll need to get beyond these influences.

Insight will come when we free ourselves, at least temporarily, from the grip of the known. Begin by acknowledging that you know very little (the less the better). Allow for the surprise and delight of the new. Willingly toss out much of what you have held on to up until now.

Above all else, listen. Listen with both ears. Listen without projecting your personal desires. Put aside all the filters through which you normally listen, and really listen.

Beyond this I can say very little. We each have to make our own way. I encourage you to slow down and begin to pay more attention to your inner states. Don't limit yourself to a one-time effort or even to a forty-day sadhana, although this will get you off to an excellent start. Rather, let this become the beginning (or the continuation) of a lifelong pursuit. Go within and plumb the very depths of your being. Listen to your soul. This work will give your life its meaning.

Scrutinize your vision, check its authenticity, doubt it. How does it really feel to you? Does it stir your heart and appeal to your soul? Have you discovered a uniqueness that must be expressed? In the most silent moments of your meditation, ask yourself this: "Must I do this?" If the answer comes back "Yes, I must," then move ahead and build a new life around your vision.

5
PROSPERITY

We've come a very long way toward our goal, the success of the soul, but we still have much to do. If you have begun to live in a more peaceful way and have at least some moments of genuine stillness, you have achieved a great deal. If you have taken advantage of this ability to quiet yourself and have begun listening to the voice of your own soul, which speaks softly but emphatically of its needs, you may have begun to receive vision, a quality even more rare than peacefulness. But if you were to stop at this point and do nothing further to fulfill your vision, your life would feel incomplete, and this, after all, would seem tragic.

We have asked about the soul's urges, of our higher calling. With our new understanding of purpose, we have a challenge before us: to devote ourselves to the tasks of the soul. Success at this mission will require that we set aside our attachments and fears, including the fear of success itself.

Success, as we will use the word here, means the process of achieving a desired result while enhancing health, happiness, and wholeness. In this sense you achieve success as you skillfully work toward an ultimate goal, even if you have not yet reached that goal. Conversely, I do not consider successful a person who has a profitable business or a high-paying job but finds herself unhappy at her work. Such people, highly stressed, unable to sleep well, and with their health deteriorating, fail at life itself even as they advance their careers. Here we will measure success in terms of the joy felt along the way as well as in terms of the goals achieved. By this measure, real success may elude us for it will require sensitivity to the needs of the soul as much as attention to worldly goals.

Wealth means an abundance of money or property, but true prosperity does not require wealth of this kind; in fact, some will consciously choose not to acquire or hold wealth. Others will want only a certain limited amount of riches. Still others will have a personal vision that includes great wealth.

Abundance is an attitude, a belief that anything can be accomplished if a person focuses enough positive energy on his or her goals. People with an attitude of abundance may achieve a great deal. Cultivating optimism, they tend to reach their goals and meet their quotas. But if they do not also have a well-developed sense of their higher purpose, they may become caught up in their success and lost in their money and accomplishments.

Prosperity is the state of having or gaining in anything good or desirable. We tend to think of prospering as having or gaining in wealth, but that represents too narrow a view of goodness. Here we will use the word *prosperity* in its broadest sense: to indicate a gain in wealth or peace of mind or anything else considered good. Each of us has our own ideas of goodness, of what prosperity means to us, of the conditions that fulfill our vision.

Real success does not come to us when we strive after it. Then we acquire only money, position, prestige, or other commodities that we might use to measure success. I do not consider these success but only its most superficial trappings. Many very unsuccessful people—people with serious personal problems, addictions, failed relationships, and so on—have acquired a good deal of money, position, or prestige, but having these things has not brought them happiness.

To take this a bit further: How could ambitious people be called successful? Their desire for more, their discontent with life as it is defines them as *un*successful. They believe that they must have more before they can feel happy. True success, on the other hand, implies a great freedom, the freedom *not* to have to go after more, the freedom to feel that you have enough. Success of this sort comes when the mind becomes quiet and gives up its self-centeredness. If you don't gain success in this soulful way, you will not find happiness despite all your efforts to grasp wealth or prestige, and your difficulties will only increase. With real success you experience no conflict, no desire, no suffering.

These types of success and prosperity are like peace and love: states without discontent, truly spiritual states.

Even given the inequities of our society, the success and prosperity we aim for is a possibility for absolutely everyone, or at least for everyone willing to prosper. But prosperity will not come easily. As with the quest for peace and purpose, the search for prosperity requires wisdom, technique, and commitment. I can (and will) communicate principles of prosperity and teach techniques for opening the self to an attitude of prosperity, but information of this sort will not make you prosper. Only you can do that for yourself. Prosperity results from ways of thinking and being as well as acting; if you have not already developed these patterns, you will need to practice them. For many of us, especially those born into poverty and those with damaged self-images, doing so may not come easily. Hardly any of us has emerged from childhood totally free of self-doubt or other scars that keep us from knowing all that we can achieve. We need to elevate our consciousness enough to recognize and root out our own self-sabotage. We need to move forward despite all the obstacles that we have put in our own path and those few obstacles that come from the outside.

❧

Before going into techniques that will help us to prosper as individuals, let us briefly focus on a few of the economic and social issues that relate to a more universal prosperity. I hesitate to make this digression but feel that I must. Too much has been written, too many courses and workshops presented, in which prosperity has been taught without regard to its potential impact. As the rich have gotten richer, the poor have gotten poorer. The environmental impact of the expanding economy has been horrifying. We can no longer ignore these facts, pushing them under the carpet of our conscience. Anyone hoping to increase prosperity in his or her life ought to consider the consequences of that endeavor.

In the modern world, large corporations control vast wealth and wield enormous power. Over the past hundred years or so, the corporation has emerged as the dominant institution on the planet. As yet, however, business has not taken on the responsibility that properly goes with such dominance. Within the culture of capitalism, we have made the tacit assumption that business, acting in the spirit of free enterprise and under the influence of market forces, would bring greater good into the world. While certainly we would not soon scorn the easy availability of food, medicine, communications technology, and the thousands of other benefits of business that many of us enjoy, in recent decades it has become clear that the results of big business are not always beneficial or benign.

The time has come for business to develop a new sense of responsibility for the consequences of its actions. As the dominant force in the world, it must consider its every action in light of its responsibility for the whole. Economic globalization has spread poverty, social disintegration, and environmental destruction; this process must be reversed before the promise of universal prosperity can be realized. Just as we need a revolution in the way that we as individuals look at the problems we face, so too do we need a revolution in business practices, a sort of ecological-spiritual revolution in which responsibility and a more spiritual connection to the rest of humanity take their rightful place alongside the quest for profit as primary motivations in business.

Our society has adopted materialism as one of its dominant values. Business tells us hundreds of times a day that we must consume, that having equals satisfaction, that we can fulfill our longings in the marketplace, that our next purchase will give us the gratification we crave. Somehow, we have evolved from hunter-gatherers into consumer-borrowers.

New values must take hold. We expend too much of our energy seeking money and the things that money can buy. We seem born to shop. Shopping and acquiring ever more substitutes for the pursuit of loving relationships, creative expression, spiritual upliftment, and other activities that contribute to the good of ourselves and the communities we live in.

Slowly we are coming to understand that there are limits to our planet's ability to handle this compulsive consumption. We have begun to recognize that other attitudes may serve our needs better than unchecked materialism, and that the void we feel might be better filled with love and strong social roots than with still more wealth and consumer goods. The results of this new thinking have just now begun to manifest themselves: The globalization of the economy has led to social, economic, political, and ecological disintegration, but recently a small but growing countertrend has begun. It promises to lead us toward the creation of sensitive, locally based, and self-reliant economic and social structures supporting people as they find their own paths to a future of their own choosing.

For this positive trend to continue and expand—and it is by no means certain that it will—two very different but interrelated processes need to take place at the same time. Through the first process, the real subject of this chapter, individuals need to take hold of their own prosperity in a responsible, loving way. In the second process, commerce must be transformed through responsible actions of government and business.

For individuals to prosper in the way I use the word, they must live consciously, aware of their own deepest longings and acting with kindness. Then their efforts and enterprises will give back the satisfaction they seek. When aware people act in the world, they create good for themselves as well as good for the greater society. We can expect that the jobs they take, the businesses they build, and their creative efforts will all have positive effects. These same people will support positive government and corporate efforts and will speak out against still more mindless exploitation. Perhaps most important, these people will serve as examples, inspiring models for those who come after them. These elevated people will help to make prosperity possible for all.

The other factor promoting universal prosperity, the part played by governments and multinational corporations as well as by smaller businesses, will happen only when enough individuals within those institutions begin to think and act responsibly. A relatively few farsighted individuals can change the vision and direction of even an enormous corporation or a powerful country. I am encouraged by a growing number of instances of enterprise with soul. Consider the World Bank as an example. In the last few years this bastion of economic conservatism, wedded to mainstream capitalistic investment, has nevertheless sprouted the World Bank Spiritual Unfoldment Society. This unofficial group of World Bank employees concerned with spirituality in commerce recently inspired the bank to sponsor an international conference entitled "Ethical and Spiritual Values and the Promotion of Environmentally Sustainable Development." This small beginning stands not alone but as one of many related efforts, a part of an emerging trend.

In order to make the changes necessary for more universal prosperity, the appetites of the rich and powerful for still more riches and power and the appetites of ordinary people for still more consumer goods must decrease. This can happen only through a transformation of consciousness. While such a transformation will have many stimuli, ultimately it too will come out of many individuals changing themselves. Then, and only then, can we begin to construct a sustainable economy that mimics nature. This kind of economy will exist to fulfill genuine human needs and enhance quality of life rather than to divert us with frivolous goods and services.

In the economy we need to build, work itself will take on a new meaning. Currently, many of us suffer a kind of emotional and spiritual death at work, a withering of our values and, in consequence, of ourselves, of our very souls. We shoulder a burden of stress that causes tremendous inner conflict. The corporation of today offers us no security, yet it demands of its employees passionate service. Questionable and downright unethical practices force us to compromise and rationalize and leave us with a lack of meaning in our lives, the feeling of wasting away. This will change only if we change, if we as leaders begin to create a new way.

In the near future profitability must be yoked to responsibility, and companies must evolve new, more kindly internal environments just as they develop better ways to relate to the world outside their walls. Hierarchies that block personal development will fade away. Management by caring must supplant management by fear. Businesses must evolve into places for learning. Corporations must become places where people like to meet. They need to create environments in which we can learn and take comfort from the example of nature. The time has arrived for a culture of soulful work based on vision, values, ethics, purpose, and other intangibles, not just on profit.

Economic forces do not have to exploit and destroy. They can restore and sustain. This requires, first of all, the transformation of individuals from blind consumers into conscious, responsible people who derive their fulfillment from progress toward their own ideals of purpose rather than from the acquisition of still more stuff. As we grow in the awareness of our own souls, we also grow in awareness of the souls of others and of the world itself. We become connected, soul to soul, with all others, and we become mutually responsible for the whole. With this sense of responsibility, we will each do our part to create an economic system that allows for universal prosperity.

Other books, by better-qualified authors, will teach us how to build a restorative, rather than an exploitive economy. I only want to declare that our work toward personal fulfillment and prosperity cannot take place on an ivory tower, in isolation from the consequences of our actions. Our every action impacts the larger world, and we ought to take this into account as we plan our futures. No program for personal prosperity that ignores the impact of our deeds will truly satisfy. Ultimately, unconscious enterprise will destroy itself along with the planet.

This brings us back to our primary purpose, to help you as you seek to give life to your own vision. If you have dreamed well and often, if you have sought growth and a purer self-image, then you can begin to abandon those old patterns and beliefs that no longer serve you. You've readied yourself to make your external reality reflect your internal vision. To move forward now will require that you let go of the old and embrace the new. For this new birth to happen, something old must die.

THE PRINCIPLES OF PROSPERITY

We become prosperous and bring into reality the stuff of our dreams when we recognize and abide by certain principles. These ways of thinking, believing, and acting open us to a flow of success and abundance while keeping us focused on purpose. As the following ten principles will make clear, we suffer no lack in the world, only uneven distribution caused mostly by our own attitudes. Many of us have learned, incorrectly, that having means taking (and hoarding), and that we face a limited supply of what we need. This sense of scarcity results, sometimes consciously, sometimes unconsciously, in fear for our own survival, and we act accordingly. In the pages that follow you will begin to reverse limiting beliefs and embrace a system of thought that will lead you to prosperity. At the same time, as a part of this change in your thinking about scarcity, abundance, and prosperity, you will understand more of your relationship to the whole web of life and how your prosperity will serve the prosperity of others and of the planet itself.

PRINCIPLE I: *You draw to yourself whatever you pay attention to.*

We are nothing more or less than our own attention. Although we *have* a body, a mind, a personality, possessions, relationships, roles in society, and so on, we *are* consciousness and nothing more. When we direct that consciousness, that awareness, to one thing or another, we tend to draw that thing toward us, to magnify it in our life. Everything that we have we have sent out a beam for.

Much of the time, we remain unconscious of what we beam for, what we draw to ourselves. We believe that events just happen to us. At other times we operate on a theory of scarcity, believing that if we want something, we'll have to struggle for it. We may think that we have to capture our share, as on a field of battle, whether we desire a lover or a new car.

Yet as we open ourselves to prosperity, neither of these belief systems proves adequate. The truth lies on a middle path, somewhere between the extremes of helplessness and aggressiveness. On this path, the path of success and abundance, you can expect the fulfillment of your needs and wishes, but you will need to take the responsibility of focusing your positive attention on them. By adopting a meditative mind, one that can one-pointedly focus on your intentions, you will open yourself to all possibilities. But if your attention remains split, with some energy going in one direction and some in another, then you will continue to draw to yourself a mixed bag of experience.

Being split in this way reflects the inner splits of our personalities. For example, if I don't find a part of myself acceptable, this part tends to get hidden away. And yet it remains, demanding subconscious attention, scattering my conscious mind, and drawing energy away from my intended purposes.

The antidote is meditation. Use it to slow down the agitation of your mind. Explore the still, silent spaces between your thoughts. Learn to recognize your reactive mind, being pulled this way and that by thoughts and sensations as well as by subtle fears and desires. See and resist the temptations of all this and then focus your attention on your life's purposes. With clear and focused attention (and appropriate effort), you will draw to yourself all that you will ever need.

PRINCIPLE 2: *Prosper so that you may give.*

You might have millions in the bank, beautiful homes, and all the things that you have ever dreamed of. But if you are unable to give and share what you have with others, you are merely manifesting the same fears that drove you to accumulate your wealth to begin with. No one living in fear can succeed at life. They won't prosper no matter how rich they may become.

We may share money, time, attention, love, support, or

anything else that we have to give. Those who give freely know that they came into this world with nothing and will leave with nothing. All they have has come to them on loan from the Infinite. Givers have confidence in the unending supply of energy they tap into and have no fear of running out.

PRINCIPLE 3: *Giving leads to prosperity.*

By giving we open up a space into which we can receive still more. Whatever you do in this world comes back to you, magnified many times over. The law of karma has become well known: As you sow, so shall you reap. Have the faith and courage to let giving become a practical tool to open up prosperity in your own life. If you only have a dollar, give a dime. It is an act of fearlessness, a statement that you trust in the Universe to care for your needs and a declaration that you do not live only for yourself.

A true gift, one given only for the benefit of the recipient, expresses love. Love given always results in love received, although not necessarily from the one to whom you originally gave your love. Giving keeps love, wealth, and other goodness in constant circulation. To covet or hold onto goodness stops the flow of it toward you. Eventually your own supply dries up, you find yourself cut out of the flow, and you stop receiving.

And yet, do not misunderstand that people give just so that they may receive. We give to express our liberated self, our soul manifesting in everyday life. To do otherwise, to hold back our kindness or our cash, cuts us off from the community of souls, and the stingy ones seem to wither slowly.

Giving can take different forms. Some gifts express affection or personal sentiment, as the giving of a present to a friend, relative, or lover. Other gifts support a cause: gifts given as grants for some special work or effort. With them we express our social, religious, or political beliefs. And, finally, with tithing, we express our faith. When we tithe we give without any sense of self-expression. This part (traditionally one-tenth) we return to the infinite source of all. We tithe with the understanding that we return to God a portion of what came from God. As our way of giving thanks, the tithe has no strings attached. All three forms of giving—to express affection, to support a cause, and to express our faith—elevate the giver.

PRINCIPLE 4: *Earn your living righteously and by your own effort.*

What consequences does your work have? Do you believe in the usefulness of your work? Do you do it in a way that uplifts others? Does your livelihood provide a real service? Do you make an effort to work in the most positive and loving way that you can?

Examine closely the social meaning of the work that you do. At some level, almost any occupation in the modern world causes some harm even as it provides a useful product or service. The poet uses energy to light her desk, and the typical farmer's produce actually contains more fossil fuel energy than solar energy. Few of us will prosper without consuming some of our precious resources. But we can make choices that minimize the harmful effects of our work and maximize the good.

Our marketplaces overflow with products and services that do nothing positive but actually degrade people or the natural world. Some (overpowered cars, for example) give people a false sense of self-worth at the expense of the environment. Much of the so-called entertainment we pay for promotes the worst values imaginable. Our culture supports an enormous trade in weapons and drugs, a good portion of it legal. If your work involves you with these kinds of products, I suggest that you carefully consider what you do. While I certainly am not saying that anyone who works for a gun manufacturer must immediately leave that job, I emphasize that we all need to act deliberately and consciously. Everything we do deserves awareness.

Our work begs for meaning. Each of us will define that in our own way and will make different career decisions at different times of our lives. But, for most of us, our ideal work should give us a way of serving others, it should provide a way to deepen ourselves through continual learning, and it should do no harm. If we approach what we do with moment-to-moment awareness and meet these simple criteria, we will find meaning in our work.

The jobs that we have may not automatically provide the needed ingredients for meaningfulness. But, in many cases, we can elevate a job with our good intentions. Once I worked in a town park, several thousand beautiful acres of Atlantic Ocean beach, and I was assigned the single task of keeping the employee lunchroom and toilets clean. All the workers gathered there before and after work, at morning and afternoon breaks, and for lunch. They always left the lunchroom a shambles and the bathroom nasty. I loved that job. I felt a sense of pride of service as, five times a day, I returned the place to a pristine condition. I observed the forty or fifty employees carefully and learned something about human nature. As I scrubbed the toilets, I thoroughly enjoyed the process of cleaning. To me, my lowly work had meaning.

If you can't find a way for your work to become meaningful, please consider your options. What does it cost you to continue in a job that you do not believe in? You must consider practical matters, of course, but beware. How many of us keep up at careers that damage our spirit, in exchange for a secure paycheck?

Principle 4 also states that we should earn our living by our own effort. Avoid exploiting the labor of employees. Provide more than adequate compensation and good working conditions if you have the power to do so. Honestly work for what you earn and do nothing dishonest.

These days fewer and fewer of us do manual labor. I consider this a great loss and view physical effort as a tonic for the spirit. Look for ways to physically involve yourself in the product or service your business provides. Clean up after yourself. Help a customer load his car. Occasionally participate in the hand work that goes into your product. Do some of the ordinary, less creative work, the work that must be done over and over again. These small things will involve you with people and help to break down one kind of limited self-image.

If you already work with your body as well as your mind, so much the better. Nevertheless, consider whether your creative and intellectual gifts are being used fully. If not, look for ways to bring these aspects of your being into your work.

PRINCIPLE 5: "*Work is worship...*" (Yogi Bhajan)

If you dedicate your work to the service of higher consciousness in yourself and others, and if you do your work without attachment to the benefits or fruits of your labors, you practice what we call karma yoga, the yoga of action. With an attitude of service, work that might have been seen as hardship or drudgery can be transformed into a delightful way of enriching our own lives as well as the lives of others. In this way work truly re-creates, providing a renewal as effective as any worship.

When we work in this way, we give deeply of ourselves. We willingly sacrifice our egocentric self (that wants to be served) and instead we serve something higher. We work so as to reflect the truth that our every act expresses the infinite working through us. In this way our work can ennoble us.

PRINCIPLE 6: *Success requires strategy.*

It doesn't matter what you want to accomplish: profit in your business, developing a new skill, becoming well known in your field. In any case you'll need to start with a strategy for success. Strategizing means facing facts and setting aside emotions and wishful thinking.

Deal with yourself and others in a way that satisfies feelings and emotions if you wish, but when it comes time to make a strategy, become more impersonal or risk making biased decisions. You need to see the pros and cons of each situation and to consider all the circumstances and factors that form the context of your strategic decisions.

Your vision will form the foundation of your strategy. In broad terms, vision tells you what to work for and strategy tells you how. If you wish to become a concert violinist (your vision), then your strategy may include practicing for hours each day, going to music school, and making contacts with other musicians.

After strategy comes tactics, the specific ways that you will follow through on your strategy. If you need to practice the violin for six hours a day, your tactics might include setting up a work schedule that will allow for that. Beyond tactics, success demands attention to detail. In music this may mean details of technique; in business it may mean the attention that assures that each customer's order gets filled correctly. Whatever you do, pay attention to detail.

Vision, without strategy, tactics, and the many little actions that they suggest, will take you nowhere. One of my students comes to mind. For years she had been unhappy living in the Northeast and had felt a powerful yearning to live in the West. She had a clear vision, but no matter how much her friends and I encouraged her, she remained stuck in her old job and her old home, unable to imagine how she would ever make her move. Finally, at a prosperity seminar I gave, she accepted the challenge of coming up with strategy and tactics that complemented her vision. I asked her what it would take to realize her dream in the next twelve months. She spoke easily enough of her vision. She even constructed a workable strategy to bring it about. But when I asked her to imagine what tactics it would take to complete her strategy in one year, all of her fears surfaced. She couldn't picture herself actually leaving her job, writing an effective résumé, or leaving her old friends behind. These tactical details had stopped her. By bringing her objective closer, by seeing what it would take for her to reach her goal in one year, the inner obstacles that had been blocking her all along became quite clear. After that we worked together as she overcame her fears one by one. Within a year she had made her move and now feels that she has at last come home.

Your vision and even your strategy may reach a high level of development, but carrying them out may be another story. Here is a simple but powerful exercise. Imagine your goals. Now imagine them fulfilled over the next five years. Now imagine them fulfilled very soon, within six months. What does that do to your thinking? What obstacles does that reveal to you? Put your attention on these obstacles. How will you go around or through them? What do they tell you about yourself or your organization? What outside help do you need, what new resources? This sort of question will come up when you formulate goals and then mentally picture achieving those goals quickly. Doing so will tell you what you'll need to do to go from wishful thinking to actual accomplishment.

Even if you plan expertly and can state quite clearly what you need to do to reach your goals, your efforts may come to nothing if you don't manage your time well. Books and programs about time management abound, but I can sum them all up in one simple sentence: Do now whatever is most important to you. Most people get bogged down dealing with unimportant details or get sidetracked by recreation or "urgent" matters that don't further their primary cause. When I write (my first priority), the ring of my phone demands my attention. That ring seems urgent, demanding attention now. So I might stop the flow of my writing to answer the phone and get involved in a conversation with a salesperson or a friend who wants to chat. After four or five phone calls, a trip out to get a few groceries and more paper for the printer, and a leisurely lunch break while I read the junk mail, my day has just about disappeared. If I care about writing, I need to put it first and keep at it until I've done all I can for the day. Then I can focus on the less important or the "urgent." If I stick to this pattern, letting the answering machine deal with the phone and doing all my errands one evening a week, I'll actually get my book written.

Strategic planning requires ongoing thought and revision. Vision endures, changing little if at all during a lifetime, but strategy must be a good deal more flexible. What seems like it would work today may prove useless by tomorrow due to new circumstances not foreseen just a little while ago. If my business plan calls for opening a second location next year but this year a competitor opens down the street from my intended location, I'll need to change my plan. Success requires more flexibility today than ever in the past. Change has become the only constant, and the rate of change is accelerating. Revisit your strategies frequently and modify them whenever necessary.

Look at your strategy and tactics every day and then brief yourself. What will you do today? Give yourself your orders and then carry them out. At the end of the day, report back to yourself. Go through a debriefing process to see how well you did, why you succeeded or not, how you would modify things the next time. Does this sound a bit too rigid to you? If so, maybe you need to be a little firmer with yourself if you expect to produce the results you want. Become willing to push past your internal, self-created blocks as well as obstacles in the outside world.

PRINCIPLE 7: *Your purpose has its own needs, which you must serve.*

In my career as a dentist, it was clear to me that my large practice had a life of its own. It had needs, it had an identity, it progressed and regressed and evolved. It had its own contracts, marketing, strategy, and so on. I could apply my own vision to the practice, but if I did not serve its needs, it would suffer. In addition to my role as key "employee," my job was to meet the needs of the practice. If we needed a new employee, I had to hire her or see to it that someone else did. If the supplies budget went out of control, I had to deal with the matter. If a patient had a complaint or a compliment, I had to communicate that to the practice. I served the practice, and much of my energy went into doing whatever the practice demanded.

This principle, quite obvious (although often neglected) in business, also holds true in other work. I have a friend who paints wonderfully. Her canvases carry deep emotion and visual beauty. But she doubts whether she should devote so much time to her work. As a result, she has held back, denying her art some of her energy and in that sense not serving her life's purpose. Her art has suffered with this lack of attention just as a child might not thrive if denied a mother's love.

We should, of course, derive personal satisfaction from the work we do or the service we provide. This remains central to the whole idea of fulfilling purpose. But we need also to recognize that to succeed, we must serve both our purpose and its vehicle. If we go into a business or a project with only an expectation of personal satisfaction, then we have a greater likelihood of failure. If, on the other hand, we moderate our personal agenda and our personal needs and serve the needs of our work, then our work is more likely to bear fruit and will grow eventually to serve us.

Sadhana, spirituality in daily life, helps us to set aside personal agendas as we go about the work of fulfilling vision. It gives us the capacity to clear ourselves of limiting desire and fear. Daily practice helps us to come to our work free of the emotional baggage that gets in the way of intuition and blocks the flow of clear thought, goodwill, and opportunity. Sadhana is one of the foundations of prosperity.

PRINCIPLE 8: *Know your motivations.*

Perhaps you know someone like my friend Julian. He began, about fifteen years ago, to develop a company that served other businesses as they upgraded their computer technology. His company provided help in purchasing, setting up new systems, and training. As the world went high-tech, his business grew exponentially. One year the company was one of the 500 fastest-growing companies in the United States, and Julian was invited to a national conference to celebrate that accomplishment. He found himself in a hotel ballroom with the CEOs of the other 499 fastest-growing companies and had a life-changing realization. He saw how unhappy many of these people were, and he knew that he was just like them. In his drive for success, he had sacrificed much of his inner peace and had ignored many of his own core values. His success had in no way served his real purpose of finding lasting happiness. It was then that Julian made the decision to sell his company and refocus his life. Today he remains active in business but takes on roles more in keeping with his most deeply held values. His new roles do not demand that he trade off his enjoyment of life for profit.

What Julian discovered was that he had not asked himself the simple question "What will my success do for me?" He had no idea why he wanted to work those long hours or why he wanted to serve at the helm of a rapidly growing business. Without a clear understanding of his motivations, he had found himself swept along by the tide of success, despite the negative effects it had on his life. We ought to question everything about our motives. We should ask ourselves over and over, "Why do I want to do this?"

Of course, some of us should run large and successful businesses. You may know with certainty that you are committed to using your success for the good of your community or that you need to create success to rid yourself of old fears and insecurities. But do exercise care. Success can be seductive, and you can wind up chasing it for all the wrong reasons. Know your motivations.

PRINCIPLE 9: *Live as your authentic self.*

Authenticity will allow you to enjoy your success. Know yourself, behind your social masks and behind your fears, sorrow, or guilt. Live soulfully. Doing so will earn you happiness. Too often we think that happiness comes from success, but it does not. Our happiness comes from authenticity, from holding to our own values, from becoming ever more self-aware. Our success should serve that authenticity. It should enable us to express our true selves. When you have built for yourself this authentic happiness, you will make others happy, and that will give you the greatest satisfaction of all.

PRINCIPLE 10: *Let go of all else and you will reach your natural state: happiness, success, and prosperity.*

We always receive from the Infinite source of all exactly, precisely, what we need. I think that this is the hardest lesson that any of us have to learn, but it is also the most valuable and the most liberating. Consider your own life. What event or circumstance do you find hardest: your job or your marriage or the death or sickness of someone you love? The difficulty acts like an arrow pointing directly to the real source of your distress, the inner fears and desires that rule your emotional life. Follow that arrow inward and eventually you will find wounds that have never healed. Here you will find your real work. Direct your self-love to this place and begin the process of healing. If you have the will, the harshest difficulties can become your greatest gifts.

At all times and in all circumstances, we have what we need for our growth and development as human beings. This doesn't mean that we have exactly what our personality wants but rather that we have what will most serve our true purpose, namely, the recognition and reclamation of our essence. If we have an emotionally difficult time with something, then we know that we have come up against a block, a place where we are still holding on to our fears. Only through the difficulty can we even recognize the existence of the block, and only then have we a chance of healing into the liberated, happy state we all desire. It is only by facing our fears—by squarely confronting our own emotions—that our growth can proceed. Thus, even our struggles serve our higher purposes.

What about the "good" things of life? These circumstances give us the time and space to reflect, relax, and rejoice. From them we get the resources we need to share and serve. By the laws of cause and effect, we draw to ourselves more of these rewards as we learn to deal in a more positive way with the challenges of life. And, of particular interest in this discussion of the success of the soul, we seem to prosper as we come to believe in the essential goodness of all of life's vicissitudes.

The universe serves us with infinite abundance. We already have exactly what we need. Now the time has come to use what we have in order to fulfill our highest purpose. This prosperity becomes increasingly accessible as we learn gratitude and acceptance and we begin to see both the pleasant and the unpleasant as gifts of equal worth.

6
THE FORTY-DAY PROSPERITY PROGRAM

Prosperity comes to us as the result of deeply held beliefs. The state of prosperity, as we are speaking of it here, exists first of all within us as a matter of consciousness. Only after the conscious and subconscious minds embrace the full meanings of prosperity and success do we begin to receive without hesitation. Success comes with fearlessness, a state free of self-sabotage and with no sense of lack. This forty-day program will unite body, mind, and spirit so that you'll begin to manifest your purpose and prosperity.

I will offer you three different kinds of techniques to use over the next forty days: specific kundalini yoga exercise sets, meditations that will alter your subconscious relationship to success, and a series of ten affirmations for you to contemplate. I will ask you to record some of your thoughts and feelings in your journal. And I strongly suggest that now is the time to consider increasing the amount of time, money, and other resources that you give back to society. Perhaps more than anything else, generosity will clear your path to prosperity.

Try to do all of these things. An ideal program would include a morning yoga set and meditation and an evening meditation plus contemplation on the affirmations and writing in your journal as well as a program of giving. I know that you might find this more than you feel you can comfortably do right now. If so, decide ahead of time what you can do, make a commitment to that, and stick with it. Later you can do another forty days using more of the techniques. Any part of this forty-day sadhana can effectively stand on its own, but if you can do it all at one time, the effects will multiply.

AFFIRMATIONS FOR PROSPERITY

In this part of the Forty-Day Prosperity Program, you will develop positive mental attitudes in relation to prosperity. They will allow you to let go of negative illusions about success and begin to claim your destiny. It takes at least forty days for new thought patterns and habits to become established. If you miss even one day of the affirmations, start again at the beginning so that you maintain perfect continuity.

Establish a specific time that you will do your practice. I like to do affirmations after meditation, when I feel most clear and open to fresh ideas. You might do it in the morning or in the evening before bed. Anytime will work fine. Mark the completion date on your calendar (and plan a little celebration for then).

In your journal, make an entry before you begin the program. In your own words, write about your resolve to create new, more productive mental habits. For example, you might state that as of this day, you choose to drop the belief in money as the only measure of success. Perhaps you'll write something to the effect that you have, in the past, held on to a belief in the power of money to fix your problems (if that seems true for you) and that you now feel ready to take back your own power. You may write something about how you have believed in the possibility of scarcity or of deprivation, of how that has led a sense of separation from the unlimited source of all. Or write how, as of this day, you intend to stop seeing yourself as a victim of circumstances and will instead acknowledge God as your true support, the true supply of all that you will ever need, and your very substance. Do all this as thoughtfully and as individually and personally as you can, letting its truth come in your own words, from your own most peaceful inner self.

Having done this, you can now begin to contemplate the daily affirmations. I have provided ten statements. Each day you will read and contemplate one of them, going through the whole list four times in the next forty days. After reading the affirmation of the day, meditate on it for fifteen minutes or more. Focus your whole mind on each part of the affirmation. Let the ideas fill your mind and your body, feeling the statement as well as thinking it. Understand it with your intellectual mind and embrace it with your intuitive mind. Notice the subtle effects that contemplating the affirmation has on your body: places of tension or pleasure. Near the end of your fifteen-minute period of contemplation, repeat the affirmation out loud six times, speaking with conviction and enthusiasm. If necessary for privacy, whisper the words so that only you can hear them.

If the words I have used in the affirmations are not just right for you—if, for example, you are uncomfortable with the word *God*—modify them to suit you. Try to avoid diluting or changing the basic message of each affirmation as you do this, but find language that works best for you. You'll want to be able to hear these words without recoil. This is not to say that each of these affirmations should be easy to understand and embrace, especially in the beginning. They are designed to challenge old notions and patterns of thought, and you may discover a good deal of initial resistance to their meanings.

Immediately after each contemplation period, write in your journal whatever thoughts come to you. Sometimes in workshops I have asked people to write, quickly and without thinking, with their nondominant hand. When we have tapped into the right brain in this way, the results have often included surprising insights. One of my students wrote to me recently to say that the discoveries she made while doing this exercise had allowed her to refocus her life completely. She had previously insisted on a career as a graphic artist, holding on to that idea with "white knuckles" even though she was getting nowhere. As she wrote in her journal with her opposite hand, fresh ideas came through and she was able to understand that she was stuck on something that no longer fit who she had become.

During these forty days, consciously strive to live according to the Ten Principles given earlier as well as by the implications suggested to you by the Ten Affirmations. Contemplate one affirmation each day for fifteen minutes or more.

The Ten Affirmations

1. I devote myself to living in this moment, fully conscious of all thoughts, feelings, and sensations. I have let go of all desire. Thus I know the constant presence of God in all, and I live in supreme peace.

2. I stay ever conscious of the inner presence of God as a lavish source of good providing all I might ever need or desire. The abundance in my life enables me to freely and joyfully give of myself and my resources for the benefit of others.

3. I love to share generously with others a part of all that I receive. I remain aware of the soul within me as my total fulfillment, and I give generously and selflessly, confident in God, as my abundant supply.

4. The soul and spirit within me energize my body and mind so I can work and earn righteously. I have unlimited energy and unlimited prosperity available to me at all times.

5. Every action of my mind and body expresses the Divine presence within. I use each moment as an opportunity to connect consciously with my God-self: my total fulfillment and the source of all.

6. I choose to devote my God-given energy to fulfilling my highest purpose. Each obstacle gives me more of what I need in order to know, love, and serve God, the soul within me, and all creation.

7. I gladly do all required of me as I carry out my life's work. I love serving the divinity that forever expands in me, and I feel gratitude as it reveals its abundant nature.

8. I live to serve the divine within me, my true identity. I let go of motivations that might lead me away from this purpose. I feel totally confident that God and its unknowable wisdom will, with my cooperation, take care of my life and affairs.

9. I trust in my own beautiful, bountiful, blissful essence. Right now, I forgive all of the errors in my life, let go of all limited ambitions, and allow my soul to shine through. I know the God in me as my unlimited supply.

10. I know my God-self as my total fulfillment and the truth of my existence. I completely relax in that knowledge and put myself into the flow of infinite energy.

God appears to me as every form and experience that I could possibly desire and instantly meets my every need.

KUNDALINI YOGA FOR PROSPERITY

The following two yoga sets will complement your affirmations and meditations. When you use them, allow enough time to go through the entire set without rushing. As I mentioned before, a good program will include one of these sets, followed by one of the meditations and an affirmation, and it will continue daily for forty days. In this time you will establish positive new thought patterns, on both conscious and subconscious levels. Because the yoga will work on a physical level, you will no doubt notice physical blocks or limitations to your practice. These can serve as useful indicators telling you where to put your loving attention. Gently stretch the tense areas using relaxation and awareness rather than force. Strengthen the weak areas over time, gradually increasing how long you do each exercise. Be gentle with yourself and avoid pain.

KUNDALINI YOGA SET FOR ENERGY AND A POSITIVE PROJECTION

Exercise 1: The Camel Ride. Sit in a comfortable cross-legged posture or on the front edge of a firm chair. Hold your shins (or knees if you are on a chair) with your hands. Inhale as you bring your belly and lower spine forward. Exhale as you bring your lower spine backward and pull your belly in (see Figures 14 and 15). Repeat at a rate of about once in two seconds. This will feel a little like riding a camel. Keep up for up to three minutes, inhaling

FIGURE 14

FIGURE 15

"Sat" and exhaling "Nam." At the end take a deep inhale, hold the posture, and breathe for about ten seconds while pulling up on the muscles around your rectum, and then relax quietly for up to five minutes.

FIGURE 16

Exercise 2: Sit with a straight spine. Interlock your fingers in a "bear grip" at the level of your heart. Inhale as you raise your left elbow and lower the right; exhale as you raise the right elbow and lower the left (Figure 16). Breathe with your abdomen, remembering your mantra. Do this moderately fast, about one breath per second, and keep up for the same amount of time as you did the Camel Ride. Use your mantra and focus at the third eye. When you have finished, inhale deeply, hold briefly, and then relax.

While you relax, continuously meditate on "Sat Nam" either silently (inhaling "Sat," exhaling "Nam") or chanting aloud in a monotone, holding the sound "Sat" for seven seconds and the sound "Nam" for one second (one repetition per breath).

FIGURE 17

Exercise 3: Sit straight. Let your head fall back (see Figure 17). Inhale deeply, exhale, and while holding the breath out, pump your belly in and out eight times. Then inhale, hold the breath in, and again pump the belly eight times. Repeat this entire process a total of three times. Then bring your head back to a normal, straight posture and relax, meditating silently on your breathing.

Exercise 4: Stay in the relaxed and meditative state of the last exercise and bring your attention to your navel area. Focus there as you breathe in and out, using the mantra "Sat Nam" with each breath. After a minute or so, imagine that your mind can lift up out of your physical body. After another few minutes, take a deep inhale, hold the breath in while you vigorously rub your hands together, and then relax and prepare yourself for one of the next meditations.

❧

This yoga set generates energy, which you may experience as heat in your body. It then directs this energy so as to eliminate tension and open you to both love and power. These exercises will help to give you the balance you need for success through service.

KUNDALINI YOGA SET FOR ATTRACTING THE POSITIVE AND FOR PROTECTION FROM THE NEGATIVE

FIGURE 18

Exercise 1: Sit with a straight spine. Block off your right nostril by gently pressing your right thumb against the right side of your nose (Figure 18). Let the other fingers point straight up. Begin long, deep breathing, inhaling with the belly first and then also expanding your chest. Stretch out the inhale for as long as you can. Exhale even more slowly, first from the chest and ending by pulling in on your belly. Aim for the longest, deepest breaths that you have ever taken, building up your lung capacity over time. The slower your breathing, the calmer your mind becomes. Remember to use the mantra "Sat Nam" and to concentrate at the third eye in this and the other exercises in this set. Keep up for three minutes or more. At the end, inhale once again and hold your breath for as long as you can before exhaling and relaxing.

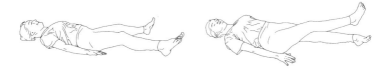

FIGURE 19   FIGURE 20

Exercise 2: Lie on your back, lift your legs six inches from the floor, and scissor them back and forth over and under each other. Do several repetitions for up to three minutes, depending on your capacity. Inhale as the legs spread apart and exhale as they cross. When you have completed the exercise, take a deep inhale and then relax completely on your back for a minute or more.

In this exercise and in Exercise 3, you must be careful not to strain your lower back. Keep your lower back pressed to the floor during the entire exercise. If you arch up in this area, you may strain yourself. Bending your knees slightly will reduce the pressure on your back as will placing your hands under your buttocks. As you gain in strength, you'll be able to do these exercises with your legs straighter and without the help of your hands, but there is no rush. Just keep practicing at the level that is proper for you, and improve slowly over time.

Exercise 3: Still on your back, inhale and lift your left leg twelve inches from the floor as shown in Figure 21. Exhale and lower it.

FIGURE 21

Then do the same with the right leg, and continue to alternate legs for up to five minutes. Imagine that you can use your breath and the mantra to lift your legs, rather than depending on your muscles. Observe the same cautions for the health of your lower back that were mentioned with Exercise 2.

FIGURE 22

Exercise 4: Without resting after the last exercise, inhale and raise both legs up six inches (Figure 22). Hold your breath and the posture as long as you are able, relax down, and then repeat, over and over, for up to five minutes. Aim to slowly strengthen the muscles used in this exercise. Again, be careful not to strain the lower back.

Exercise 5: Still lying on your back, bend and raise your knees. Put your arms over your head on the floor, hugging your ears with your upper arms and keeping your arms straight (see Figure 23).

FIGURE 23   FIGURE 24

From this position sit up, extend your legs, and touch your toes, keeping your arms by the side of your head (Figure 24). Do this as you exhale. Inhale, and lower yourself back into the starting position. Do this a total of six times. Then lie back down and relax for as long as you wish. Then sit up for your meditation.

MEDITATIONS FOR PROSPERITY

MEDITATION 5:
MEDITATION TO BRING PROSPERITY

You can do this very sweet meditation for any amount of time; just three minutes several times a day will give you a wonderful break from your routine. Try this instead of a coffee break or before an important meeting. It will help keep you focused on your higher self and your higher intentions. If you wish you may extend the time up to a half hour or more and work this meditation into your morning or evening sadhana.

To practice this prosperity meditation, sit straight, either on the floor or in a chair. Close your eyes and mentally focus your attention at your chin. Doing so enables you to understand yourself, to see yourself more clearly. Or you can have your eyes just slightly open and look, without blinking, down at the tip of your nose. Focus this way if you want to lock your mind and keep it from wandering as you meditate.

Then take a long, deep inhale. Expand your abdominal muscles first and then expand your chest to take in a full breath. While you hold the breath in, mentally recite: "I am bountiful, I am blissful, I am beautiful." Then exhale slowly and completely and hold the breath out while you mentally recite: "Excel, excel, fearless." Continue to repeat this for the duration of the meditation. At the end, take one last deep inhale, hold the breath for a few moments, and then slowly exhale and allow your breath to return to normal. Sit still for a moment longer before opening your eyes and continuing your day's activities. If you do the meditation for an extended time, you may want to sit still, breathing normally, for a bit longer before getting up. Use this time to do nothing, just listen with heightened awareness to your own inner self.

Consider some of the many times during the day you could do a few minutes of this meditation. Do it while waiting for a bus or before leaving the parking lot for the trip home. Do it whenever you can and keep reminding yourself of your real self. "Beautiful," "blissful," and "bountiful" apply not to your personality but to your soul. They reflect your true nature. By repeating them, you bring attention to the soul in you, to your divine self. To take this one step further, keep the mantra going even when not sitting in a formal meditation. Imagine the effect of saying to yourself "I am bountiful, I am blissful, I am beautiful; excel, excel, fearless" over and over, with each breath, throughout the day. To practice in this way, just let the mantra stay in a part of your mind as you go about your other business. You can do this when you walk the dog, do the dishes, even while watching a movie or during a conversation. Eventually it becomes an automatic thing. Fall asleep with the mantra in your mind, wake up with it, let it guide you through the day, helping you to keep your priorities in order.

MEDITATION 6:
PROSPERITY MEDITATION FOR SELF-RELIANCE
(TAPE 2 SIDE 2)

When Yogi Bhajan taught this meditation in 1978, he said that Guru Nanak, the founder of the Sikh faith, had taught it in India almost five hundred years ago. I always feel delighted knowing we practice techniques passed down by the wonderful sages who came before, preserving these teachings as a legacy to us. Now we will use them as we reclaim our own spirituality, and in turn we will pass them on to generations yet to come.

This meditation will allow you to have an experience of your soul. Our religions have taught us to have faith, to live by the rules, to not question, to believe. But dogma and superstition cannot substitute for real religion. Religions also have given us moral codes to follow. We can do that, we can live with morality, but behind all the morality we still have to deal with the self. We have to find out the truth of our own existence because ultimately only that matters. That is true religion.

It doesn't matter how much money we have or how devoted we are to family and friends, for all of that will come to an end someday. Nothing matters but knowing the truth, knowing God, knowing ourselves. Belief won't do that for us; belief won't give us that experience.

In practicing this meditation, you can have a direct experience of you, the real you. With that experience, with that knowledge of your self, faith becomes superfluous. That does not make religion superfluous; rather it makes it real religion, religion based not on fear and blind faith and beliefs that give false security but religion based on experienced reality. This meditation will serve you. It will help you to experience yourself and thus to believe in yourself.

So many of us, living and working in modern society, come to define ourselves as what we do instead of what we are. We have difficulty separating our identity from our success or failure. Our self-confidence goes up and down with our fortunes. We run after success, desperate for the feeling of potency that we think success will give us. This meditation will help you break that pattern. By building a deep sense of self-reliance and helping you feel your real potency, this meditation brings success. It gives you confidence in your own ability to create and produce so that your actions will bring about the effects you want. With it you will let go of wishful thinking and replace it with concrete action. This meditation will help you to become productive.

FIGURE 25

Sit in a comfortable posture with a straight spine. Close your eyes almost all the way but allow just a little light to come in. Your vision will go into soft focus. Hold your right arm so that the forearm is in front of your chest, parallel to the ground, with the palm facing down. The right hand winds up just in front of the center of your chest. Position the left arm so that your left hand comes to shoulder level, palm facing forward, as if you were taking a pledge. Bring the tips of the left thumb and index finger together, with the other three fingers pointing straight up as shown in Figure 25.

Then take a deep breath and chant the mantra

Har, Har, Har, Har, Ha-Ree, Ha-Ree

"Har" and "Haree" refer to the creative aspects of God. Pronounce the *r* sound in "Har" with the tongue striking the palate. Each of the eight syllables gets equal stress and one beat. After the eight sounds you should have used up all your breath. Take another breath in and begin again. One repetition of the inhale and mantra should take about ten or fifteen seconds minimum. With practice you may want to slow down the breathing and chanting still further. This will help you relax even more. Continue the meditation for eleven to thirty-one minutes. When you have finished, take a deep breath in, hold the breath for a moment, and then exhale but continue to sit perfectly still for a while longer. During this very quiet time, suspend all thought and simply listen.

❧

I encourage you to explore all of these techniques. Each will work on a different aspect of you. They will free you from old patterns of wishful thinking about prosperity and enable you to take charge of your own destiny. But don't take my word for it; experience it for yourself.

7
A FINAL WORD

This book has had but a single purpose. With it I have endeavored to share with you some ideas and methods for elevating consciousness. I have tried to go beyond philosophy and give you the means to excel. The more challenging task is now up to you. You need to apply these techniques in your own life. In the beginning that may not prove so hard, as starting takes only a moderate measure of inspiration and a tiny leap of faith. Later on it may become more difficult. When you have meditated and have felt the effects of the meditations, then you must decide if you actually want to follow this path. More precisely, you must decide if you will continue to apply the methods, on good days and bad, when you want to very much and when you can't stand the idea of it, for change will take that kind of perseverance, that ability to keep up.

I have seen many, many people, people with the most sincere desire to lift themselves up, who have not kept up, even after they have tasted of the nectar of peace, purpose, and prosperity. Why is that? What makes it so hard to let go of the old ways and begin a life of self-love? Some of those who have dropped by the wayside have done so because they have tried to conform to someone else's idea of what will save them: some dogma or belief system. But this cannot satisfy our deepest cravings. The one who conforms can never really flower. We need freedom to flower, freedom to be our own authentic selves, freedom not to conform to another's standard.

Others have failed to keep up because they have rejected their own emotions. Eventually we need to be free from the harmful effects of negative emotions such as lust, anger, greed, pride, attachment, ambition, or avoidance, but freedom never comes to the person who tries to get rid of these emotions. It comes only to the one who recognizes them in himself or herself, and, recognizing them, acknowledges and accepts, even honors, their presence. Whenever the mind, with its cunning and fear, tries to become something other than itself, it loses all chance of real success.

So you have before you a simple task, even though I fear that you will try to make it difficult. You do not need to go after something that you do not now have, you only have to touch something already there. Let go of all your desires, even the desires concealed in your sweetest prayer, if you intend ever to reach the source of peace and love. No book can teach you about this source; no one can lead you to it. Good works (although necessary) will not take you there. Only when your mind cultivates serenity and freedom from ambition and motive, only when it wants no more and no less, only then will the source of love and peace stand revealed before you.

And so we have come full circle. We began with peace and we return to peace, our natural state. Along the way we have taken a most risky path, going into realms of purpose and prosperity, realms where even now we might easily become lost in thickets of ambition and desire. And yet we have to tread this path if we dare to hope for a life of fulfillment. We have no other way.

Sat Nam.

CASSETTE CONTENTS

Tape 1

Side 1
Prelude
Guided Meditation into Who You Are
Postlude

Side 2
Prelude
Guided Meditation for Vision
Postlude

Tape 2

Side 1
Prelude
Mindfulness Meditation
Interlude
Meditation for Peace
Meditative Silence
Postlude

Side 2
Prelude
Meditation for Emotional Clarity
Meditative Silence
Interlude
Prosperity Meditation: A Meditation for Self-Reliance
Meditative Silence
Postlude